work smarter, not harder

A PRACTICAL GUIDE TO PRODUCTIVITY

GRAHAM ALLCOTT

This edition published in the UK
in 2018 by Icon Books Ltd,
Omnibus Business Centre,
39–41 North Road,
London N7 9DP
email: info@iconbooks.com
www.iconbooks.com

First published in the UK
in 2014 by Icon Books

Sold in the UK, Europe and Asia
by Faber & Faber Ltd,
Bloomsbury House,
74–77 Great Russell Street,
London WC1B 3DA
or their agents

Distributed in South Africa
by Jonathan Ball,
Office B4, The District,
41 Sir Lowry Road,
Woodstock 7925

Distributed in Australia and
New Zealand
by Allen & Unwin Pty Ltd,
PO Box 8500,
83 Alexander Street,
Crows Nest,
NSW 2065

Distributed in Canada
by Publishers Group Canada,
76 Stafford Street, Unit 300
Toronto,
Ontario M6J 2S1

Distributed in the USA
by Publishers Group West,
1700 Fourth Street,
Berkeley, CA 94710

ISBN: 978-178578-332-6

Typeset in Avenir by Marie Doherty

Printed and bound in the UK by Clays Ltd, Elcograf S.p.A

About the author

Graham Allcott is the founder of Think Productive, one of the world's leading productivity training companies. Think Productive works with a diverse range of organizations including eBay, the Cabinet Office (UK Government), the National Trust, BT, American Express and the Bill & Melinda Gates Foundation, running workshops that help their employees beat stress and develop playful, productive momentum in their work. He is also the author of the internationally best-selling book, *How to be a Productivity Ninja*.

Graham has worked on a number of charity and social enterprise projects in various roles including employee, founder, CEO and chairman.

Despite an intolerance of failure elsewhere in his life, Graham is an Aston Villa FC season-ticket holder. He lives in Brighton, UK.

Author's note

It's important to note that there is much frequently-used research employed in the areas of productivity and time management.

Where I know the source, I have been sure to reference it, but my apologies here to the originators of any material if I have overlooked them.

Contents

Introduction

Welcome to *Introducing Productivity*, a practical guide designed to help you in your work and life. Improving your productivity can sound like a daunting, annoying and maybe even vague goal. There are holy grails that it feels like you can never reach and oh-so-perfect colleagues and friends to enviously compare yourself to. It's difficult to know where to start, particularly when you're so overloaded with things you have to do that you don't even have the time to think about productivity, let alone make changes. But of course, when you're feeling like this is coincidentally when you most need to improve your productivity!

The purpose of this guide isn't to take you painstakingly through your day working on every bit of it, but to give you quick tips that will make a difference. That's why I've written it as an A–Z. After all, one thing we all have in common is that there are so many other things vying for our attention; so while I recommend you do read this book from start to finish the first time, it's also something you can dip in and out of whenever you need a productivity boost. Some of the things you find here might be a refresher, while other things may be totally new. And while naturally a lot of the advice I'm giving focuses on working life, many of the ideas are equally applicable to your home life, your hobbies, etc. – you name it, it can be done more efficiently.

You may be wondering about my definition of

'productivity' and who this book is really for. Put simply, if your work involves such a level of thinking and complexity that there is more than one way you can tackle your day, then this book is for you. And if you're stressed, deal with a lot of complexity or ever feel like you need to be more organized and in control, then this book is definitely for you.

You may also be wondering who I am to tell you about productivity. Well, I know first-hand what a struggle it can be to become really productive. I'm naturally disorganized and unstructured, but a few years ago, close to burnout and realizing that working for myself meant I had no one to delegate it all to, I decided to kick my own productivity into shape. It became something of an addiction and inspired me to start my business, Think Productive, which teaches productivity skills to some of the world's leading companies. I also wrote a best-selling book on the subject called *How to be a Productivity Ninja*.

I will talk some more about the 'way of the Productivity Ninja' in the N is for Ninja chapter later, but suffice to say, if you'd like to learn how to practice Zen-like Calm, become more Agile and Prepared, be more Ruthless with your focus and be Weapon-savvy with all the various tools that you have available, then that's a chapter that you can't afford to skip!

Although you may strive for perfection, I firmly believe no one is perfect at productivity – it's something that you need to constantly work at. Change can come from trying new things, but can also come from revisiting, refreshing or reinforcing good habits. Truly mastering something that you were previously really good at can give your productivity as much of a boost as trying something completely new. So keep an open mind and don't be afraid to dip in and out, cover the same ground twice, or skip bits to return to later. Focus on the bits of this book that either most excite you *or* most repel you. My experience is that a bit of exhilaration and excitement is important when focusing on changing your habits, which is ultimately what 'improving productivity' is: good habits, skills and behaviours.

Of course, in a small book like this, it's impossible to give you all the answers. But actually when it comes to productivity, it's impossible for any book of any length to provide all the answers. A big part of mastering productivity is recognizing your personal preferences – positive and negative – and realizing that certain rules or principles that work well for you might not be the things that work for someone else, and vice versa. You see, Productivity Ninjas are human beings, not superheroes. They have foibles and failings, they screw up sometimes and they can't be perfect. Yet with a little work on fostering the right habits, skills and behaviours, they can often appear as effortless and magical as a superhero in their work!

So this book will start with the assumption that you're human – and I hope it gives you a chance to reflect on the way you work. Whatever the work you're engaged in, I hope you can use this book to help you focus on the stuff that matters, get more done with less stress and develop a playful, productive momentum in your work and life.

A is for Attention

This book is an A–Z of productivity. Luckily, the word 'attention' begins with an 'A', so despite the potential constraints of such a format, it's possible for us to begin at the very beginning.

There used to be a thing called 'time management'. The idea was that your productivity was affected by how you spent your days: the literal management of the 9 to 5. But the term 'time management' itself is deeply flawed, and those old time management techniques, with their rigid systems and paper diary planners, don't work anymore. We live in a technological age where rapidly changing priorities are no longer a distraction but actually part of what we have to manage.

So we're going to begin this book at the beginning. You can't manage time. There's no point trying. What you *can* manage is your attention, and it's an even more subtle skill to learn. There are several layers to consider here in *how* you manage your attention, like managing the interaction between your attention and the information you need to do your work, managing your *habits* and how they affect your attention, managing your stress and eliminating distractions to give you *more* attention and managing your body and mind to give you *better quality* attention. Through this book we'll look at mindsets, organizational structures, technology, habits, psychology, nutrition and all the practical stuff like email and meetings ... but at the root of it all is how to manage and optimize your attention so that you have your attention on what matters most to you and what makes the most difference to your work and best serves – without wanting to be grandiose about it – your contribution to the world.

The new mindset of knowledge work

Your attention is a more limited resource than your time. Have you ever got to the end of a day where you've still got loads to do, you're still motivated to do it and you have all the tools or information that you need, yet you're still just staring into space? Under those circumstances, you'll often tell yourself you ran out of time, but actually you just ran out of attention.

On other days, you might be in back to back meetings all day, and it's 4pm before you even have a chance to get any desk-time in, to finally look at emails, catch up on your reading and planning, and seize control. On these days, you might really feel that you're short on time. But if you start to think about, what you're left with at the end of the day is a small amount of time but an even smaller amount of attention: you had energy and ideas and brain power when you were sitting in all those dull meetings, but now at nearly 5pm, there's not much of it left.

The demands on your attention are far more than the demands on your time. An hour-long meeting can (usually!) only last an hour and you can set the beginning and end points in your calendar quite reliably, yet an hour spent working on a complex project can throw up so many other things that can try to grab your attention, with all the processes, risks and stakeholders to manage and all the ideas and possibilities you may have for the project. Likewise, you may sit down to what you think will be an hour of answering useful emails, only to be rocked off track by other people's priorities popping up in your inbox. And we haven't even talked about the option to check social media or browse gossip on the internet when you're bored, because obviously you're far too disciplined to succumb to such distractions!

Pay attention. Wisely. Time might be spent, but attention still needs to be paid. Look after this currency, as it's the most valuable currency in the world.

Managing attention is both art and science

There are loads of things we will cover in this book that will help you manage your attention. I like to think of productivity and attention management as both art and science.

The science bit is in the organizational structures, the use of tools and technology, the building on what you know has worked in the past (for you and for others) and in maintaining a regular 'feedback loop' where you spend some of your attention being conscious and mindful around your own habits and analysing what's working for you and what's not. When most people think about 'productivity' as a subject, they think about the science stuff. They read productivity websites that have articles called things like

'Seven great new android apps' and 'What Mozart knew about productivity'.

Yet the 'art' of attention management and productivity lies in finding your own personal formula for getting into a state of what psychologists call 'flow' and what Buddhists call 'Zen': the ability to be present, in the moment, focusing your attention only on the one thing you want to focus it on. Most people experience this fleetingly, usually in moments where you're up against a deadline and that deadline means you forget your hunger, you forget the other 10,000 things you could be doing at that moment and you're 100 per cent engaged in the work. Or you experience it because you're in a crisis and there's one thing that's so big it commands all of your attention. But it is possible to reach this level of Zen-like calm regularly in your work – you just need to make some effort eliminating distractions. (We'll come to that later.)

The art of attention-based productivity is personal, less predictable and in some ways unique to each of us. In her book, *The Artist's Way*, Julia Cameron talks about creativity being like an 'inner child', and we know what children need: protection, nurturing, motivation, food, teaching, safety, to be listened to, to be treated as an individual and to be free from stress. So one key productivity lesson is to learn to be a bit kinder to yourself. The truth is so many people are quick to beat themselves up when things don't go their way, but a cycle of 'stress, lower productivity, more stress, even lower productivity' isn't good for anyone. Our instincts and sense of guilt often favour the stick not the carrot.

TRY IT NOW!

Far from the opposite of being productive, being kinder to yourself is integral to keeping the show on the road and to you continuing to feel great and perform well in your role. So list three simple steps that you're going to take that will allow you to be kinder to yourself. It could be as simple as leaving the office on time every day this week, booking your next holiday, treating yourself to a relaxing, full-hour lunch break, having a massage or even just vowing to stop checking your emails when you're not in the office. Whatever you choose, make a commitment to these choices by adding them to your diary or to-do list. And stick to it!

We will focus later in the book on the whole concept of Zen and the idea of staying 'in the moment' with your work. It is a subtle art, but one that can transform your ability to deliver the ideas and the work that really makes a difference.

Quality attention

The reason that attention is such a key facet of productivity is that distractions can only be eliminated to a certain extent. We can control to a large degree how and when we allow email to distract us, but for most of us, the idea of not having email at all isn't an option. So our thinking process that leads to productivity must start with the question: 'Can I be sure that what I'm working on right now is the most appropriate thing for me to be doing at this exact moment?' Of course, there are a number of variables to take into account when answering this question, but here's the biggest and most overlooked: your level of attention available.

Attention is a more limited resource than time. Everyone is different, but typically you may find that you're better prepared to do your best work earlier in the day, or maybe you're someone who's terrible in the morning but comes alive at 4pm. As well as having an idea of the times you're on form, you probably also know the times in the day that you're the least capable of meaningful work. You know the drill: make coffee, scroll emails, look busy. Again, we're all human and our job isn't to strive to become superheroes, our job is to work with what we've got.

Broadly speaking, I like to think that the quality of my attention falls into three distinct categories or levels:

1. Proactive attention
These are the times in your day where you're fully focused, fired up, feeling fresh, in the zone and ready to tackle the most complex of tasks. Most of us will have no more than two to three hours of proactive attention in a day (and also typically more at the start of the week than the end).

2. Active attention
These are the times when you're plugged in, ticking along nicely, not quite at your best, but competently engaged with most things. Most of us will spend the majority of our day in this active attention level.

3. Inactive attention

These are times when you're flagging and your brain feels a bit fried. Perhaps you've been at work too many hours or perhaps it's too early in the morning to tackle the hard stuff. Or maybe you're feeling a bit foggy after that high-carb lunch.

Of course, these are crude and artificial demarcations, but it's vital that we develop an awareness of the relationship between attention level and the complexity of our work. Scheduling tasks for your day or your week based on your attention level – and reacting in the moment based on how you're feeling and what new things are emerging – is the only way to get anywhere near close to having a good answer to the question: 'Can I be sure that what I'm working on right now is the most appropriate thing for me to be doing at this exact moment?' Because attention – particularly your proactive attention – is truly the most precious resource you have at your disposal.

It's important to note that everybody is different. We all have different preferences and biorhythms. For me, proactive attention is usually from 9am until mid-morning, and then I get a second burst in the afternoon. In recent years, I've also learned what's good and bad for me to eat for lunch to avoid the inactive attention lull that I used to experience in the hour or so after lunch.

TRY IT NOW!

What does your attention look like during typical day for you? When are you at your absolute best (proactive attention)? When are you flagging (inactive attention)? And what's the bit in the middle? Write out a timetable of your attention levels, and see how it fits with your current work schedule. Could you organize your day to use your attention levels better?

Increasing your proactive attention

Finally, in this very brief introduction to attention management, let's think about how we can get more of it! And specifically, wouldn't it be lovely to have an extra couple of hours of proactive attention each day? Unlike time, which is a constant for everyone, there are ways to increase how much proactive attention you have at your disposal.

Firstly, you can make sure your brain gets all the fuel it needs to function at its best for as long as possible each day. (We will look at the wider topic of food, the body and productivity in the chapter J is for Juice.) Physical activity and good nutrition go a long way to keeping you at your best for longer.

Secondly, you can turn lots of little moments from your day-to-day life into surprise moments of productivity – but you do need a little forethought to do this. For example, think about how much time you spend travelling to and from work, sitting in waiting rooms or on flights, standing in queues in the supermarket or just walking along the road.

So much of this time can be used really productively, creating whole new pockets of attention. (Later in the book we'll look at lists and how you can use them to enable you to take advantage of these surprise opportunities for productivity.)

- You can't manage time but you can manage attention.

- Unlike time, attention isn't a fixed resource, and an hour of proactive attention is far more valuable than an hour of inactive attention.

- It's important to think about the quality of our attention and aim for Zen-like calm: that state where we're interacting only with the thing in front of us, in the moment, and are not thinking about lots of other distractions.

B is for BHAGs and Batching

BHAGs

In 1961, John F. Kennedy made a speech in which he said: 'This nation should commit itself to achieving the goal, before this decade is out, of landing a man on the moon and returning him safely to the earth.' It felt astonishing, brave, visionary and, let's face it, a little unlikely. Yet within a decade, it had happened. After Russia put the first man into space just a few years earlier, the Americans rallied their resources behind this grand vision and made it happen. It was an example of a 'BHAG' – a Big Hairy Audacious Goal.

The term **BHAG** was coined by James Collins and Jerry Porras in their 1994 book, *Built to Last: Successful Habits of Visionary Companies.*

So Amazon's BHAG is 'every book, ever printed, in any language, all available in less than 60 seconds'; the charity Habitat for Humanity's BHAG is 'a world where everyone has a decent place to live'. In the 1960s, Nike's BHAG was simply 'crush Adidas'.

Five years ago, my personal BHAG was to have the best-selling book on the topic of productivity and to create a productivity company that comes top on Google search in the UK. Now I'm aiming even higher, because it's useful for your BHAG to feel just a little bit too big, to be out of your direct reach – it's designed to stretch you. Think Productive's new BHAG is to be the biggest influence on workplace productivity and work/life balance in the world.

What makes a BHAG different from a simple vision statement or corporate plan? Well, a BHAG is emotionally engaging, with a chance of success but also an element of uncomfortable jeopardy. A BHAG compels the people in your organization or team to rally behind it, with the sense that together we could achieve this, but only if we *really* focus on it. It becomes the driving force behind your corporate plans, and while no one remembers most of what's in a corporate plan, it's almost impossible to forget a BHAG.

Whether you're leading an organization, arranging a family event or setting about a new project, then it's vital that you have something audacious and tenacious to help drive you forward. Whatever your circumstances, the notion of BHAGs can help you to think about your bigger picture and provide the motivation you need.

What's your Big Hairy Audacious Goal? Take a few moments to remind yourself of your current goal, or to think up a new one. Make sure you write it down and put it somewhere you'll be reminded of it regularly.

In trying to define your own personal BHAG, you might like to think about the following:

- What are your values?

- What most excites you in your work and life?

- What is the best use of your skills?

- What does the world most need from you?

Your organization's BHAG and you

It's important to stay motivated in your work, and work becomes much more fulfilling when you see an alignment between your organization's BHAG and your own. Being clear about your goal and your organization's goals gives you the momentum to keep going when things get difficult. This alignment of their BHAG and yours could be a direct alignment of passion, whether that be for fitness, solving world hunger, technology products, or anything else that you're passionate about. Or it could simply be that you know your role in the organization and know you can help, but your mutual BHAG is based more around you and your organization earning a good living.

It's important here to think about the unwritten rules of work because they're important factors in staying motivated and ensuring a fruitful partnership between you as an employee and your organization. Of course, if you're self-employed and you *are* your organization, this is even more vital!

Your employer pays you to create some value for them. The more value you create, the happier they are. But there's also a need for you to get some rest, have a life outside of work and feel appreciated and respected by your boss and team.

I believe that factors such as technology, transparency and the changing work population will lead over time to more flexible 'deals' between employer and employee. We'll move away from the set-hours culture to more flexibility and a blurring of the lines between work and life. We'll also begin to move to a more outcome-based measurement of success and professionalism, rather than the old-fashioned system of simply measuring whether you were in the office for the required number of hours.

If done well – that is to say, if you are able to develop a good rapport with your organization and manage your work like a partnership – there are huge benefits to increasing productivity and having a happier working life. (Since you're reading this book I'm assuming that you're someone who is motivated to achieve more in your work and for yourself – and that feeling less stressed in your work would be useful to you.)

 What are the unwritten rules in the relationship between you and your organization? Think about:

- Your organization's BHAG and how it overlaps with your own

- How much flexibility and trust you have with your boss

- How receptive your boss or team would be if you suggested different ways of working that might make things easier.

Batching

If you think about any activity you might need to undertake, from writing a report to filling in your expense claim, or from conducting research to planning a meeting, the scale and scope of the task is much easier to contemplate when you're underway than it is before you start. There's a certain set-up time required to get into the mindset of writing a report or compiling your expenses. You need to remind yourself how the systems work, line up the right documents on your screen or get the paperwork in front of you. This set-up time can be a barrier to productivity or even a root of procrastination. Often, the set-up takes as long as the task itself – think about how long it takes to key in all the security information you need to access your online banking versus how long it takes to actually make the bank transfer. Yet once you're in the zone with something, it's quite easy to keep going.

Batching is a technique to reduce this set-up time and help you to stay in the zone. The idea is simple: store up similar tasks into batches, so that you do lots of them less often rather than more regularly as individual tasks.

There are lots of ways to work in batches. Here are a few you can try:

- Save up the filing you need to do into a tray on your desk. Only complete the filing once that tray is full.

- Save up invoices that you need to pay and do them once a week or once a month rather than as they arrive.

- Turn on your email, process it to zero, then turn it off again.

- Buy things in bulk – anything from buying the year's birthday cards for your whole family from a card store through to stationery supplies for the office. Stocking up means fewer trips to the shop or less time spent on the website fiddling around for your credit card verification.

- Set up meetings and schedule travel at the same time each day. I don't schedule new meetings or calls until the end of every day. My diary is pretty complex, so getting into the mode of understanding my schedule is a big set-up cost just to schedule one lousy meeting. So, if I receive emails asking me about dates or looking for my availability, I save them in a folder all day so I can deal with it all at 6pm before I finish work.

- Think about projects. Batching together all the thinking needed to keep projects on track and doing this just once a week provides amazing clarity and saves a huge amount of time otherwise wasted stressing about the status of different projects.

THINK ABOUT IT The batching approach applies outside of work too. Why not think about batching when:

- Ironing your clothes – it's much easier to do extra shirts when you're already ironing than to have to get the ironing board out again tomorrow!

- Cooking – it takes just the same effort to make ten portions of chilli con carne as it does to make two!

Can you think of any other things in your life you could try batching?

USEFUL TIP When looking at the things you might be able to batch in your job, think about the stuff you find fiddly, frustrating or boring. Usually somewhere in there, you'll find fantastic opportunities for batching, as well as some great ideas for things to do when you're experiencing inactive attention.

C is for the CORD
Productivity Model

Your job is not your job.

There is a fundamental difference between the kind of job you might have had in the pre-digital age and the kind of job you have now as a knowledge worker. In the industrial age, your job was to perform a function – think packing boxes in a factory or serving drinks behind a bar. Your job as a knowledge worker is to deliver the right outcomes and information in much the same way as someone behind a bar needs to deliver a good beer. But that's not really your *job*. That's not the bit they pay you for.

What you're paid to do is work out what the job is, how it should look, how to go about it, and so on. What you're paid to do is take information from other people's emails and priorities, react to what's happening in the wider world, apply professional expertise and define the work. What you're really paid for is the *thinking process* that goes on. After all, anyone could type and send that final email signing it all off if they were told exactly what to say!

How strong is your CORD?

My book, *How to be a Productivity Ninja*, uses the CORD Productivity Model, which we developed through my company, Think Productive, and have taught to thousands of

CAPTURE

CAPTURE & COLLECT

 Nags & ideas

 Phone

 Conversations

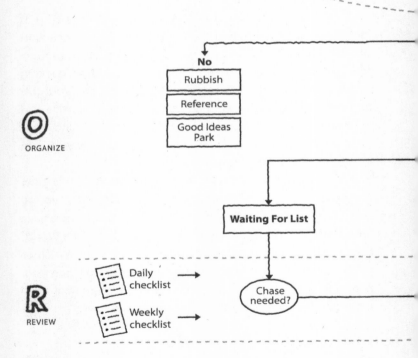

O

ORGANIZE

No

| Rubbish |
| Reference |
| Good Ideas Park |

Waiting For List

R

REVIEW

Daily checklist →

Weekly checklist →

Chase needed?

DO

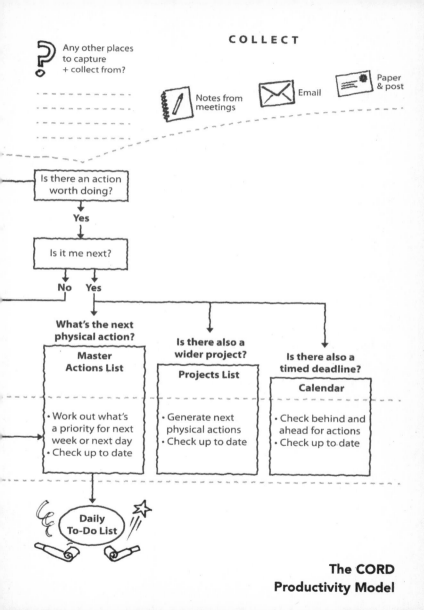

COLLECT

Any other places to capture + collect from?

Notes from meetings

Email

Paper & post

Is there an action worth doing?

Yes

Is it me next?

No   **Yes**

What's the next physical action?

Master Actions List

- Work out what's a priority for next week or next day
- Check up to date

Is there also a wider project?

Projects List

- Generate next physical actions
- Check up to date

Is there also a timed deadline?

Calendar

- Check behind and ahead for actions
- Check up to date

Daily To-Do List

The CORD Productivity Model

people in organizations around the world over the last few years. It's an illustration of 'information workflow': the journey that you go on with any piece of information, from receiving it to its final conversion into something that's either done or not done.

There are four stages to this process: Capture and Collect, Organize, Review and Do. To improve your productivity, you must focus on the habits that support each of these four stages. Think of it like a chain – one weak link will affect its overall strength. Your productivity is only as good as the weakest of these four crucial elements. So in this chapter, I'm going to run over these four distinct parts of our work and the habits that will help you develop what we call Ninja Productivity.

We'll start with a quick run-through of all four habits and what they mean, as what's most important at this stage is understanding the basics. Later on in the book, we'll focus on the tips and tricks that will aid these four habits. So if there are elements on the diagram you don't understand yet, like the 'Master Actions List', 'Projects List' and so on, don't worry, we'll come back to all of those things later.

1. Capture and Collect

Much of our stress in knowledge work comes from uncertainty about the extent or meaning of our commitments. The quickest way to breed such uncertainty is to pile up your email inbox, keep all your ideas in your head rather than write them down, pile up your paperwork so that you have no memory of the potential commitments that lie inside all those papers and be unsure about the exact demands or deadlines set by colleagues or your boss. Cue that feeling of 'information overload' and panic.

So to stop this from happening and to start you on a path to productivity, your first job is to develop the habit of Capturing and Collecting: in other words, getting everything you're working on out of your head and either onto paper or into some kind of app. The same goes for email – work out straight away what it means. Delete the stuff that doesn't have any meaning and keep the stuff you need to do something with in a folder, not in your inbox (more of which later!).

 At this stage, it's not important what you actually do with the information, simply that you trust that you'll come back to it and do something with it. That's all your brain needs to stop stressing out. Trying to remember everything you need to do, or worse still, not knowing everything you need to do, is a sure route to inefficiency and stress.

The stress-busting effects of perfecting the art of Capturing and Collecting information are not to be under-estimated. Most people know this intuitively – if you think about the times you've felt really overwhelmed at work, you probably made a list or a mind map and felt better afterwards. By that point you hadn't organized or done the things on that list, but at least you could start to see the wood from the trees and you trusted you could make progress. That's all you need to get started.

Think about what's on your mind. All those things you have to do or look into or figure out. Grab a stack of paper and a pen and write down everything you can think of. Give yourself about half an hour for this. Don't skip anything. You'll thank me later.

---

2. Organize

The Organize part of CORD is where we make sense of everything we've just Captured and Collected: all those emails, all those bits of paper, all those ideas ... They must all go through the same organizing process.

The journey to the next physical action

The language we use with ourselves really matters. It's important to get clarity on every single item on your desk, every single piece of paper, every email and every thought, by asking the simple question: 'What's the next physical action?' The idea of this question is that it's easy for tasks or projects to get stuck, or for it to become unclear what the next step you need to take actually is. If you have paper on your desk, or things that need mending or projects you still haven't started despite thinking of them a really long time ago, one of the best things you can do is stop and think about the next physical action. Have you actually defined what it is you need to physically *do* next?

This thinking serves two vital purposes. Firstly, it helps stop you getting distracted by thinking about such actions when you're trying to focus on something else, because having thought about it and stored the actions away for safe-keeping, your brain knows it can stop nagging you about it. Secondly, your to-do list is full of tangible things you can actually do, rather than the vague 'nags' that we tend to write down when we first think of them as we're Capturing and Collecting.

Imagine looking down this to-do list:

- Saturday
- Report deadline!!
- Expenses
- Anniversary.

All of these things look unclear, intimidating and difficult to *start*. So make it easy for yourself. Here's the same list articulated as next physical actions:

- Call Nathan and ask him the plan for Saturday
- Write a list or mind map of the chapter headings for the report
- Empty receipts from my wallet and drawer and compile spreadsheet
- Talk to Chaz about what she'd like to do for our anniversary.

The same items, articulated as next physical actions, suddenly feel easier to get going on. Often the psychological gap between the 'nag' (the reason it's on our minds) and the next physical action is the thing that stops us from making progress. Bridging that gap can be profound.

The Organize process is really just about asking good questions of yourself about each of these items, to define the next physical action and get really clear on the detail of when and where it needs to be completed. Is there an action worth doing here (and if not, do I want some kind of reminder of this information later)? If there's something to do, is it my turn next, or can I wait for someone else to move this along? What's the next physical action I need to take to get it moving? Is there a wider project I want to keep of track of here? And is there a deadline I need to track on my calendar?

These are simple, common sense questions. But there are some really killer benefits to practicing and perfecting your use of the Organize habit:

1. It ensures that you have a framework to get unstuck on any item that you might feel stuck on. As long as you follow this process, you'll never have a reason to procrastinate by not knowing what to do next.

2. It creates immediate momentum. When your list is full of tangible next physical actions you can actually do, it's easier to stay in the zone and get on with things

3. It creates a structure to your lists, so you always have a place to put useful information that you know you'll be able to come back to and find later.

4. It gives you a profound sense of clarity and perspective to be able to look across a complete picture of all of your projects, actions and commitments. Perspective is power!

5. The more you practise using it, the more you start to develop a laser-like focus on what matters in your work. When I coach people to use these techniques, it often feels clunky, unwieldy and even counter-intuitive on first glance, but use for a few days and it starts to become second nature, and in doing so, it eliminates so much procrastination.

 Take some of the things you wrote down in the Capture and Collect exercise. Use the CORD model to follow the Organize questions: 'Is there an action worth doing?', etc. Remember that the kind of 'nags' and ideas we write down are rarely phrased as next physical actions, so be very specific in the language you use to write down each action. Make sure you can picture yourself doing the task – where will you be; what will you be physically doing? It's from this clarity that we build momentum (a concept we'll return to later).

---

3. Review

It's no good getting everything in order during the Capture and Collect and Organize phases if you don't then spend some time working out what your best strategy is as a result. A regular review of what's on your lists can ensure you feel calm and in control – it's totally possible to be overloaded but not overwhelmed! I recommend keeping a daily and weekly checklist to facilitate these reviews (just so that when you have some time to review everything, you are being thorough and asking yourself the right questions). I will go into loads more detail in the Weekly Checklist chapter, later in the book.

4. Do

Once you have Captured and Collected, Organized and Reviewed all your information, this is where the magic really starts. Doing all that thinking up-front leaves the doing itself remarkably free from any thought at all. You are free to choose things from your list, work on one thing at a time and spend as much of your proactive attention as possible in the moment, no longer focused on all the things you're waiting to do, can't do or haven't got around to yet, but solely on the thing you're working on. It's incredibly liberating to work in such a way, and it builds really positive psychological momentum.

Using CORD to overcome 'information overload'

Recognizing these four distinct phases of knowledge work can be a great help when we're faced with the feeling of 'information overload'. Using CORD, you can work out where the 'blockage' in your workflow is and which element of the CORD process have you neglected.

Is it down to too much information coming in? Is it too much information remaining undefined and disorganized, with no sense of the potential meaning or outcome? Is it because you need to take a step back and revisit priorities and see the bigger picture? Or is it that the time for thinking is over and you need to knuckle down and clear the decks by simply getting on with delivering on your commitments?

CORD can act as a diagnostic tool to help you put your attention in the right place and become motivated and in control again.

The psychology of doing

Aside from not sticking to CORD, the other thing that can seriously harm your productivity is fear. Even when we know exactly what we need to do (a problem that CORD solves), we're often still left with the problem of our own fear of failure. We resist the difficult conversations which will make us unpopular or where we'll feel uncomfortable, or we put off writing the presentation that has so much riding on it, even if when we think about it objectively we know we have a good chance of doing really well. Yet thinking objectively when you're scared of the outcome of something is so, so difficult. So, we'd rather do anything else in the world than do the thing that matters, precisely because it's the thing that matters.

We resist the work for several reasons, but it really boils down to three things: we resist things that are scary; we resist things that are difficult; and we resist things that are boring or uninteresting. (I will return to this theme when we look at Foibles, Procrastination and the Ninja mindset.)

Again, productivity is partly an art and partly a science: some of these emotional responses to our work can be pretty complex and most of us don't really spend anything like the time we should exploring what's going on in that complex brain of ours. Usually what's going on subconsciously in our brains is a combination of 'way more than you think', 'hmmm, not pretty', and 'fear-driven freak-out', so it helps to really pay attention to our own minds as a key component of managing our productivity.

D is for Decision-making and Distractions

Decision-making

Whether you like it or not, and whether you have a boss in your job or not, you *are* your own boss.

What the CORD Productivity Model shows is that we deal with four distinct habits: Capturing and Collecting information, Organizing it so that we know the actions and projects that need to be completed versus the things that don't need to be done, Reviewing our workloads and Doing the actions.

Let's think about that in the context of the role of a boss who decides what work needs to be done and how, versus the role of a worker who does their job based on following instructions. Of these four habits, two are the traditional realm of the boss, while two are the traditional realm of the worker:

CAPTURE & COLLECT: This is when you're in your 'worker' role. You're collecting information and getting together everything you need, but at this stage you don't have to make any 'boss' decisions about what to do with it. You're identifying that there are new things happening around you – problems to solve or opportunities to take advantage of – but you've yet to think through how to react.

ORGANIZE: Now you're the boss. How are you going to arrange the information you've collected? What action is needed, by whom? By when? It's time to get your proactive attention going and make some higher-level decisions.

REVIEW: Still in boss-mode, it's worth remembering – regularly – that there's much more that you could be doing, outside of what's emerging right at this moment or the newest actions you've defined. So are you making good prioritization decisions about which work should come first, next, later and last? And more generally, are you happy with the way things are going? Should your worker-self be prioritizing differently?

DO: Finally, you're back in worker-mode. With everything organized and your plans clearly laid out by your boss-self, you can just knuckle down and get on with actually *doing* things!

When both the boss and the worker are you, it's so easy to get distracted by the doing when you should be making decisions, and so easy to be distracted by more decision-making when you need to be doing!

Separating thinking from doing
One of the most important productivity skills you can cultivate is to draw firm boundaries between the thinking and the doing. For this to work, it helps to imagine you have an alter ego: your boss-self will handle the Organizing and Reviewing while your worker-self has the Capturing and Doing all under control.

Embracing this makes decision-making more focused and makes being a worker a liberating experience too. Indeed, a focus on one thing at a time is a wonderful way to avoid feeling disorientated, overwhelmed and stressed.

 Decision-making can be hard work. So, here are a few things that might help your boss alter ego to make better decisions:

1. Make any old decision! Usually, no decision is worse than the wrong decision. A lot of decisions can be corrected or reversed later. But sitting on something because you're not sure of the answer? That's a bad move. There's an old Yorkshire saying which is: 'you get a third of your decisions right, a third wrong and a third don't matter anyway!'

2. Hofstadter's Law says: 'It always takes longer than you expect, even when you take into account Hofstadter's Law', so keep this in mind when making decisions about scheduling or timing.

3. Compromise. You can have your project delivered to maximum quality, you can have it done quickly *and* you can have it done cheaply ... but you can't have all three at the same time. Choose one of these three things to compromise on.

4. Parkinson's Law is that work expands to fill the time available. Sometimes we have to remember that our

worker-self is a slack bum who likes to surf Facebook instead of doing any work. So Parkinson's Law for me is a great reminder that sometimes a deadline will force the best bits of work out that bit quicker. Which leads nicely to number five ...

5. The 80/20 rule. In deciding where a project's parameters are, it can be tempting to get caught up in bells and whistles, or in making something as perfect as it can possibly be. Really, 20 per cent of the effort and time produces 80 per cent of the value. So know when to stop tinkering – your 80 per cent might be someone else's 100 per cent anyway.

Distractions

Much of our best work – the quality thinking and quality doing – happens when we're able to fend off distractions and keep our attention on the things that matter.

There are two types of distractions: external and internal. Let's start with those external distractions that we have to battle with on a day-to-day basis. I'll start with this thought: If you could design a more interruption-filled, uncomfortable, judgement and stress-fuelled environment specifically for the purposes of keeping someone off-topic and unproductive, you'd design something that looks much like the average open plan office. If you're unfortunate enough to work in an open plan office, then many external distractions can't be controlled. However, what you *can* do is:

- Turn off email and social media notifications so that your screen, phone or tablet is not constantly flashing new pieces of information in your face. These interruptions may feel small individually, but added together they take out a huge chunk of the day's attention.

- Take some time in your week when you purposefully work somewhere else in the building, away from bosses, colleagues, email inboxes and the like. Even two hours a week spent 'going dark' – absent from view but using your proactive attention to focus – can be extremely valuable.

- Spend some time plugged in but offline – you don't have to have your email inbox and phone switched on the *whole* time! Again, even at your desk you can control the distractions at source to some extent.

- Pay attention to how much information you are exposed to, both outside of work and in the rest of your life. Watch less TV; choose not to read the free newspapers; take some time off the internet; be 'screen-free' for a day or all weekend. The downside to our instant information culture is that it distracts us from the present moment and from our own thoughts. It's important to give your mind a rest and a chance to wander once in a while.

- Meditate. We will cover this later when we come on to Zen, but these final couple of points are not disconnected from work productivity. In fact, they're absolutely essential to maintaining good proactive attention.

Even harder to deal with than those external distractions are the internal distractions: the little voices and vices inside your head. Yes, it was you that retreated from the challenges of that spreadsheet to go and check the BBC website. Yes, it was you that spent time on that shiny new thing instead of following through on that more valuable but scary thing. There's no one else to blame (and yes, I'm just as guilty of sabotaging my own work too!).

Why does this happen? Well, put simply, lots of distractions give the illusion of having value. So when we're stuck or struggling or feeling frustrated we tend to look for some kind of instant gratification.

Low-grade useful stuff we procrastinate with:
- Checking email

- Checking notifications

- Internet 'research' into topics that in reality we don't need to research at all

- 'Catching up' with the news (which we'll read, hear or watch later anyway)

- Making *another* cup of tea or snacking

- Optional meetings

Downright useless stuff we procrastinate with:

- Solitaire/Tetris/Angry Birds/Minesweeper/Candy Crush (delete according to your device and generation)

- Office gossip

- Loops of videos or celeb gossip online – usually justified with some kind of 'five minutes of chill time' internal dialogue

The scourge of presenteeism and the case for remote working

In the BHAGs chapter I talked about the idea of the unwritten rules of the relationship between employer and employee. The issue of trust and autonomy is a critical component of productivity. In organizations that are low on trust, the issue of 'presenteeism' can be a huge problem – your ability to manage your own workload and work around your best and worst attention is scuppered or dictated by the need to be seen in the office later than your boss, or to be around purely to put in the 'face time' that seems to be noticed more than the results.

Even if you don't work in an environment where presenteeism is an issue, it's often difficult to broach the subject of working from home. Working from home, certainly in the UK, still carries a stigma, where it's seen as a slacker's paradise. Rather than seeing it as taking advantage of focused and uninterrupted thinking space away from the office, some bosses think it's just an excuse to go home and get the house tidied up, while occasionally dipping into the email inbox to give the impression of prodigious productivity.

Certainly, the term 'working from home' tends to allow the word 'home' to linger in people's minds a bit too long, whereas phrasing it as 'remote working' can help keep the emphasis on the work and help persuade your boss that you're serious about managing your attention most effectively, rather than getting the washing on or playing with the kids on company time. The general perception of remote working and more flexible working is improving over time; so, perhaps now is your chance to raise the subject for the first time and become a pioneer! Of course, it's not possible for everyone, but remote working can give you a huge attention advantage.

The scatter-brained, lazy you vs the ingenious, motivated you

We generally know what's good for us and what's not. Yet we don't always follow through in making changes to our habits and behaviours.

Productivity is a battle. It's a battle between the two different versions of you. In the red corner is the clever, motivated you. You want to get things done, you know what's healthy and what's not, and you know what you need to avoid. In the blue corner is the lazy, scatter-brained you.

The lazy, scatter-brain in you loves nothing more than gawping at YouTube for short-term gratification and forgetting to do important things. The lazy, scatter-brained you enjoys nothing more than lounging around doing absolutely nothing. There's no motivation and no will power.

Your job as the ingenious, motivated you is to recognize that part of you is lazy and scatter-brained and that, left to its own devices, this part of you will screw things up. So your job is to 'trick' this part of you. You might do this already. You might already leave your wash basket next to the front door so that you remember to put the washing on before you leave the house, or you might leave your keys on top of your packed lunch in the fridge overnight so that you don't forget your lunch in the morning. I've heard hundreds of stories of similar tricks, all of which boil down to your brain in ingenious, motivated mode taking some form of action to override the inevitable lazy and scatter-brained mode that's coming.

So when you're dealing with distractions, take action on behalf of the scatter-brained, lazy version of you. Simply trusting yourself to be connected to the internet but not to check it is naïve – disconnect it for an hour and see how much more you get done.

Remember, self-control is overrated. Relying on self-control suits the narrative of ingenious, motivated you. But it plays right into the hands of scatter-brained, lazy you.

E is for Email Etiquette

Email is one of the banes of productivity. In the Inbox Zero chapter, we will look at the personal survival aspect to email, but before that we're going to focus on the things that you do that make email easier for other people and the things that they do that make it really annoying for you. So this is about the interdependency of productivity and the culture of teams and organizations – and what you can do improve it.

We all get the email we deserve

Nothing tells you more about the culture of an organization than the way people 'do' email. It differs tremendously from one organization to the next, from those organizations that rely almost solely on it, to those that use email more as a follow-up tool but do their best work away from their inbox. Then there are those organizations where it's become the norm to be connected via smartphone 24/7, 365 days a year, and others where the thought of emailing on a Saturday would be ridiculous.

Whatever your email culture, there are things you can do that make everyone else's job easier. And why would you want to spend more than a second doing that? Well, because there's a good chance that they'll return the favour and consider you in their email communications too, and together you can build a healthier email culture.

10 ground rules for good email etiquette

1. Create momentum through clear, action-orientated emails

This sounds pretty obvious, but you have no idea how many emails I see in the course of our coaching where there is no clear action specified, and the recipient is forced to play an elaborate guessing game working out why they have received it or risk looking foolish in front of their boss or colleagues for not knowing.

2. Make your emails easy to read and process quickly – use bullet points and paragraphs

In case you haven't caught up with the rest of us, we've all stopped reading every word in our emails – there doesn't seem to be the time and, well, it doesn't seem like a particularly worthwhile activity either. So, we skim read our emails instead. What this means is that to write effective emails, you have to assume that unless you make it easy to read, it may not be read at all. Bullet points are a great way to:

* Get a number of quick points across easily

* Substitute a paragraph for just key words, phrases or actions.

3. Use people's names in the text of an email

Bearing in mind that people are skim-reading the emails you send them, including their names will help draw their attention to specific information for them. I will often start an email with an opening paragraph or sentence that explains what I'm trying to achieve, and then follow it up with short messages, such as:

> Mary: could you take a look at this please and let Sam know your availability for next Tuesday?
> Sam: could you arrange an hour in my diary for me and Mary to catch up on this?

4. The art of a good subject line

Subject lines, especially on mobile devices, are critical to the speed and ease of processing email. A good subject line is to be treasured, appreciated, applauded and learnt from. Here are some examples of bad subject lines:

> Re: fyi
> 2 things
> Urgent
> RE:
> Great news!
> Tomorrow
> Status update
> How's this?
> Need a favour
> Question

The problem with all of these subject lines is that they require further investigation – you have no idea what information is 'for your information (fyi)', no idea what the '2 things' are, and so on. A bad subject line is one that leaves you to do all the work.

So here are some good subject lines:

2 minute action pls – could you …

FYI only – the policy doc I mentioned

Agenda and map for away day, Friday 1st November @ head office

Invitation: launch event next Tuesday

Urgent: information for tomorrow's mtg – please read carefully

---

 Think about some emails you've received recently. How many had bad subject lines? And how did that affect the efficiency with which you responded to them?

---

5. Only one topic/issue per email

I know this seems like a counter-intuitive idea because in the last section I was bemoaning the volume of emails people receive and here it seems I am saying 'Send three separate emails rather than sending one email about three things.' But yes, that is exactly what I am suggesting, and with good reason. The point is not simply to reduce the volume of emails you send and receive, but to reduce the time and attention spent on them. A big part of that time and attention is spent working out how to deal with them, where they go next and keeping it moving. It is much easier to receive three emails when you know that two of them can be dealt with right away, and the third you'll need to wait on some more information before responding, than to receive one email containing all three questions.

In this instance, what will often happen is that one of the questions will fall between the cracks, and either get missed or need to be clarified later when it might have become more urgent. As a result, you'll have spent a lot more time and attention on it than if you had separated each issue in the first place. So give everything its own little box, separate from everything else, and able to be dealt with as such.

6. Keep it short

It's good to keep your emails short. If I'm trying to convey a lot of information, I try to put that information in a report or a word document briefing instead of writing a huge long email. It will be easier for the recipient to read that way, and will probably look more professional too. There's even a website that you can add to your email signature that explains why you're choosing to keep your emails short: www.five.sentenc.es.

7. Don't use email to get angry or get even

Have you ever found yourself in the middle of blazing row over email? Have you ever got to a point where you're spending far too much of your precious attention on working out whether you should make that particular sentence into capitals or whether to add a full stop here to really make that point very strongly indeed? I have been guilty of this in the past, and I am sure you have too.

The thing is, when two people are going hammer and tongs to out-do each other through the medium of words, it's extremely unlikely that one of them will suddenly stop and say: 'You know, actually, the way they have crafted that sentence means I'm inclined to agree with their point of view.' It doesn't happen like that, and the angry email chain can be responsible for the loss of an inordinate amount of attention and energy. It can be very distracting too, as you wait for the next instalment to arrive rather than getting on with any other work.

The truth is, we often do this because while a five minute difficult phone call might be much more productive, it's a lot harder to stomach than a couple of hours wasted crafting several angry emails, even if the emails end up making matters worse. So, pick up the phone. Or talk to your boss about what you should do, rather than responding to their latest delivery of electronic vitriol.

8. Don't hide behind email when communicating bad news

There are many examples of people being made redundant by email. Email can often be a great 'capture' tool, to provide a reminder of the main points and key information, but conducting such processes by email alone is a very sad state of affairs. It indicates bad management, led by cowardice rather than any set of reasonable values. Email is a great medium, but it should never replace meetings or other forms of verbal communication in a manager's repertoire. Be the bigger person and say what you've got to say, eye-to-eye.

9. CC with care

The carbon copy (CC) dates back to a time before email, where documents were duplicated using paper containing carbon filings, similar to the forms you sometimes still get in banks or on the receipt books of small cafes and restaurants. The trouble is, making carbon copies back in the day was actually a bit of a nightmare, whereas adding ten names to the CC bar on an email is pretty easy to do. It's just so available. The abuse of the CC button is probably the biggest cause of excess email I have observed, and the 'reply all' button just reinforces it. But it's easy to see why they've become such popular tools:

- People are scared to act without permission, and it allows for a certain passing of responsibility to those CC'd (usually more senior and typically their line manager).

- People like to keep other people 'in the loop' in the hope that doing so keeps them off their backs or negates the need to communicate directly with them separately to the email.

Obviously there are times when it is a useful tool, so I am certainly not saying abandon it. But before you use it, just think of the extra work you're creating for those having to process it, and ask yourself if it's really necessary. At the very least, tell people why they are CC'd if there's even a small chance they might not know.

10. BCC with extreme caution

If CC should be used with a little care and discretion, BCC is to be used under extreme caution. It's often known as the devious button, and for good reason. Its most common use is to 'privately' CC in a boss or other colleague so that they're in the loop on what's happening without the recipient(s) realizing that this is the case. Of course, if said boss then decides to hit 'reply all' when they reply to you, your cover is blown, and everyone on the To and CC bar receives their email response, knowing that you were skulking around with your boss in the background. It's easily done, and can be very embarrassing. However, BCC *can* be a good tool, particularly for protecting email addresses on 'mass' emails or so that no one knows who else is receiving a particular email (great for marketing emails, bidding processes and so on).

Talkin' about a revolution ...
Facilitate some conversations that utilize the knowledge and experience of your people,

and you'll be surprised by how exciting and productive your emails can become. Here are five questions you can ask your team members over lunch one day, over a coffee or in a brief workshop:

1. What do you recognize in yourself and in others as bad email habits?

2. What do you recognize in yourself and in others as things that make it easier for an email to get *processed* at the other end?

3. What would be the three kinds of email bug bears that you would want to stop receiving if that were possible?

4. What ground rules could you collectively set up to make these things happen?

5. When will you measure and reflect on the success of this, and how?

F is for Foibles and Frogs

Foibles

One of the difficult things about a lot of management techniques and theories is that they try to teach you how to be perfect. It can be intimidating reading what seem like simple rules while simultaneously realizing how far removed you are from the reality of the perfection being portrayed. So this chapter is about human frailties, foibles and fallibilities. This chapter is about failure. And this chapter is about fear.

Do you ever sit and wonder when you're going to be found out? Are you waiting for someone to tap you on the shoulder and say: 'You're a fraud, we've just realized it'? Do you cower at home the day before you're due to make a big presentation? Do you worry what your boss thinks of you and whether what you're doing is good enough? Well, I have some news for you. You're not alone. Everyone has their demons. Next time you're in a room with colleagues, just take a moment to look around and say to yourself, 'everyone in this room has struggles I don't know about.' The world is a much kinder place – and a more productive place – once we start to honour those struggles.

The natural way of being at work isn't human. Your boss approaches you, you have a load of work on your plate already, some emails that you just read are going to result in more fires for you to put out, and you're all set to stay late.

Then your boss plonks a huge piece of work on your desk with minimal notice. What do you do? Do you want your boss to think you're a fallible human being who can't take the pressure? Or do you view this as another chance to be a superhero? The truth is, too often, we enjoy the superhero narrative. It's glorious in that moment – that moment before we realize we don't actually have special powers.

So the idea of bringing your real self to work – the idea of being human at work – is something that I've tried to cultivate in myself and in my team at Think Productive over the years. Why? Well, I think it's healthier, more authentic, more productive and less stressful, and it leads to deeper and more enlightened communication.

In celebration of being human

Considering some of the remarkable things that human beings are achieving in your organization, in companies you admire and in life generally, what's magic is that none of it is actually magic. None of those people were actually super-heroes. Behind their success there are just as many foibles and fallibilities as any other human has. You don't need to be perfect to have success; you just have to be human.

Think about this simple question: what would it mean to be more human at work? Are there times when you've been tempted to take on more work than you can handle to reinforce the impression that you're some kind of superhero? Are there times when you have neglected your own sleep, food, fitness or health because you're under pressure?

In his book *Now Discover Your Strengths*, Marcus Buckingham argues that the overriding focus of schools, parents, workplaces and society is to work on correcting weaknesses and being well-rounded, but when schools or organizations focus instead on building strengths and specialism, they achieve better results. His research suggests that most people (73 per cent) use their key strengths only about once a week, whereas fewer than 12 per cent of people use their strengths every day.

This would echo the classic 80/20 rule that 20 per cent of what you do makes 80 per cent of the difference in terms of value, and vice versa. So actually, the whole idea of trying to iron out your weaknesses is little more than wasted energy at the periphery of adding value. The much smarter thing to do is to develop a role for yourself that plays to your strengths as often as possible and, if you're managing people, to find ways for them to do the same. Cultivating and celebrating the diversity of teams is much more than just a nice thing to do – it's a critical factor for success!

Fear and resistance
Now I'd like to look at one of the biggest productivity killers. It's nothing to do with being organized or whether you

have the right apps, and it's one of our most basic human emotions: fear.

Why do we get scared at work? Again, think back to what we're taught in school. The school system is designed to breed loyal employees, not leaders and certainly not disruptive entrepreneurs. And yet there has never been a greater need for more innovation and different ways of doing things. We even have a word now for people who shake things up from inside companies: the 'intrapreneur'. And yet school teaches us to comply, blend in, show up on time and follow the rules. We are taught that stepping out of line is scary.

At work, we rationalize that standing out and daring to be different, creating work that will be judged by others and having the courage of our convictions will lead to failure, rejection and before we know it, personal bankruptcy. Our brains take us straight to unrealistic worst-case scenarios. And yet often feeling fearful is a good indication that we're breaking a boundary and doing some work that matters. As the old saying goes: 'There's no such thing as failure, only feedback.'

Frogs

Brian Tracy's classic book *Eat That Frog* focuses on one of the consequences of our fear – procrastination. We all have tasks and activities that might be necessary but not fun. We might fear the social awkwardness, the potential for rejection, the potential for things to be hard or the potential for us to get things wrong. His advice is simple: start the day by 'eating a frog' – by doing the most difficult thing on your to-do list. This is a powerful piece of psychology.

Firstly, think of the inefficiency of procrastination. Procrastinating about something means thinking about it over and over again, constantly reminding yourself that you're not doing it, while simultaneously distracting yourself with this thought and taking yourself away from whatever else you might have been trying to do. And you keep coming back again and again to how bad you feel about avoiding something. It's a huge waste of time and mental energy.

Secondly, by starting the day by 'eating that frog', what happens is that you know that nothing else can phase you that day. You've started the day with your hardest thing, so the rest of the day is like free-wheeling down a hill. Psychologically, beginning with the heavy lifting and getting it out of the way is a wonderful feeling.

Thirdly, by building a habit for regularly confronting the things that are hard, you become more comfortable with the fear. You start to see the results that come from confronting fear.

 Which tasks over the last few days have been your 'frogs'? Which ones did you procrastinate over the most and why?

Frog momentum

It can be hard to develop the right routines or habits to make this happen. Starting the day thinking too much about that frog can leave you less and less likely to do it. One way around this is to build 'eating the frog' or 'worst first' into a wider daily habit. Keeping a simple checklist that includes your morning exercise or meditation, your breakfast, your daily to-do list planning *and* eating your frog can help establish a daily ritual that sets your frog in a wider and more positive context. The frog is just one of several things you do to honour and give thanks for the day and get you set on a good path. No big deal!

So many people focus on apps and systems when it comes to productivity. They spend time too much time organizing their stationery into neat sections and developing intricate filing systems. But how we deal with our own fear and foibles is absolutely critical to establishing good productivity habits. Without the right mindset or the ability to coach and manage yourself, there'll always be something missing.

G is for *Getting Things Done*

There's been a long history of seminal books about the subject of time management. In the 1990s, the biggest book was Stephen Covey's personal development bible, *The 7 Habits of Highly Effective People*, which I'll cover in more detail later on. Covey was the last of the traditional time management teachers, releasing his book just before the advent of email as an all-encompassing business tool.

In 2001, David Allen's *Getting Things Done* became the book of the noughties. He was the first to suggest that the approach to getting things done should be primarily bottom-up as opposed to top-down. Previous great writers on core themes like personal development, leadership and time management always start with the 'visioning'. The common ground running through so many self-help books is that you start by picturing your goal or defining what you're trying to achieve. From there, you work backwards, from life goals through to annual goals through to quarterly targets all the way back to defining 'what shall I do today?'

Getting Things Done turned this on its head by asking: 'What's on your mind?' This simple insight that for most of us, getting clear on current commitments is the first step towards achieving the bigger vision – or even being able to see the bigger vision at all – was one of the reasons I think *Getting Things Done* had such success.

KEY FIGURE **David Allen** was born in 1945 and grew up in Louisiana, USA. He is the founder of the David Allen Company, one of the USA's best-known productivity companies. His most famous work is *Getting Things Done*, although the more recent book, *Making It All Work*, is actually the one I would recommend if you have yet to read any of his work.

Below are some of David Allen's key messages that I've incorporated into my working life.

The two-minute rule

Getting Things Done advocated the use of the two-minute rule. Simply put, if you come across something and the next action takes less than two minutes, just do it straight away. The two-minute rule is extremely effective for a few different reasons:

1. It means you don't need to spend time adding it to a list and then time in the future re-reading it and trying to remember it.

2. It keeps your lists shorter.

3. It obviously keeps a lot of things moving.

4. The two-minute things are often the fiddly and annoying things, so forcing yourself to do them straight away saves a lot of procrastination.

5. It creates the positive psychology of completion, which is rare in so much of our work these days.

Mind like water

The aim of getting clear on your next actions and having a complete list of everything you need to do is, Allen says, part of developing a 'mind like water'. How does water react when you throw a tiny pebble in it? How does it react when you throw a huge boulder in it? The answer is the same for both: appropriately to the input. Nothing more, nothing less. As such, creating a good system and being clear on your commitments allows you to react appropriately when new things come along. Without this, there's always a danger of panic, or a chance that you might miss something.

Horizons of focus

It's often thought that because *Getting Things Done* focuses on the next actions and clearing your mind from the things immediately in front of you, it's somehow not concerned with vision or purpose. Allen addresses this with his 'horizons of focus' theory. These are the different perspectives or lenses through which you view your work and life. He uses the metaphor of a plane, as follows:

- 50,000+ feet: Life purpose
- 40,000 feet: 3–5-year vision
- 30,000 feet: 1–2-year goals

- 20,000 feet: Areas of responsibility
- 10,000 feet: Current projects
- Runway: Current actions

Allen's view is that you need to have an eye on each of these six horizons of focus. Each affects the others, so you need to make sure you have some level of clarity on each, otherwise you may still feel stressed.

Looking at those six horizons, you may already have existing habits and behaviours in place to focus on these. But, arguably, few of us spend enough time thinking about our higher purpose, even though it may be a topic we revisit occasionally.

Three to five-year vision and strategy is also something that may be less familiar to many, unless you have particular reasons or excuses to look at that timeframe (such as a limited contract in your job, a plan to move cities before your kids go to school or a specific course commitment).

New Year's resolutions are probably the most obvious comparison to the 1–2-year goals, and I suspect that's the one that most people would say they're regularly engaged with.

The 20,000 feet and even 10,000 feet horizons are often institutionalized – things like staff appraisals and team plans or status meetings at work will focus on these horizons – but again, I'd argue that there's a difference between thinking about it occasionally and looking at it more systematically. Finally, whether you're drowning or swimming freestyle, most people spend plenty of time at the runway level.

TRY IT NOW! Think about your own horizons of focus. Do you spend the appropriate amount of time at each horizon? Which one feels the most neglected?

Ubiquitous capture

Your best ideas can strike you at any time. You need to be prepared so that you don't lose them and also so that they don't pop back into your head again and again at inconvenient times.

Thinking back to my idea of 'lazy, scatter-brained you' and 'clever, motivated you', you need to make it as easy as possible for scatter-brained you to capture ideas – on the move, at your desk, in your house, even in the shower! I am personally a big fan of paper notelets, which I keep on both of my desks (in the office and at home). So whenever I have an idea at my desk, I have it captured and can get back to what I was doing, without the need to think about it any further. Similarly, when I'm out and about, I have an app in my phone that can quickly take down the information. In fact I have two: I use Captio for the really easy stuff, and Toodledo if there's a little more detail. The reason for that is I can use Captio without needing to focus on my phone much, so if I'm having a conversation with someone, it saves there being too much of an interruption. Both apps save the idea and keep it safe there until I 'empty it out', which I do every few days.

H is for Habits

Taken on its own, the information in this book is useless. There is simply no point in buying or reading books like this one unless you plan to actually put these ideas to good use. It's when you begin to use the information in these chapters to change your habits that the whole subject of productivity comes to life.

So why do so many people buy books like this and never even read them? Or buy books like this and read them for extra knowledge, but without actually making any change? Well, one reason is that it takes a lot of self-awareness to be able to analyse and change your habits.

The whole subject of you and your habits is most likely not what you wanted to read about – people want 'tips', 'hacks' and 'shortcuts'. You wanted secret magic formulae to make it all better. Sorry to break the bad news to you, but there's no magic shortcut, no secret formula. The only way to make lasting change is to make the effort to change your habits.

The four-stage model of competence

The four-stage model of competence offers us a window into our own minds. It details the process of taking any piece of information or new skill, from something that we can't do for love nor money right through to a learned habit or behaviour. The model suggests that we go through four distinct phases as we learn:

1. Unconscious incompetence
2. Conscious incompetence
3. Conscious competence
4. Unconscious competence.

Unconscious incompetence is when you look at somebody doing something and say: 'Wow, how do they *do* that?!' You can't do it and you wouldn't know where to start if you were asked to try. It's like when you see a juggler or magician and their skills just amaze you (unless you happen to be a juggler or a magician …).

Conscious incompetence describes the period in which you're learning something new and failing. As you learn, you keep screwing it up, but at the same time you're starting to analyse for yourself where competence could come from. You're starting to see what you'd need to do to get good at it. Imagine you are learning a new language, and the sentence structures and some of the vocabulary are coming together. When your errors are pointed out, you kick yourself and say, 'Oh no! I knew that!'

Conscious competence is where you reach that point where you can *just about* do it. It requires some effort to stay on top of it, but you can do it. It's like your driving test – you can't think of anything else in the world at that moment, other than 'mirror, signal, manoeuvre, mirror, second gear, third gear, mirrors, MORE MIRRORS! CONCENTRATE!'

Finally you have **unconscious competence**. How do you ride a bike? Well, it's just like riding a bike. It's just *there* as a habit. You don't really remember what it was like to *not* be able to do it and when you get back on a bike after a long time, you may be slightly rusty, but you don't anticipate falling off. You don't need to think too hard about it at all; in fact, it's so habitual you can think about other things as you ride along. You can check out the scenery or think about your lunch.

The reason why learning new productivity habits is so hard is that it's *not* like learning to ride a bike. We don't start from a position of unconscious incompetence (as you would if you didn't know how to ride a bike at all) but with engrained habits that already work to a certain extent. So, having the strength to jettison those habits completely and go back to conscious incompetence in order to learn a better way of doing things seems like more hassle than it's worth.

But here's the thing. If we're really honest with ourselves, we can all get a bit better at the habits that we take for granted. And with a little bit of awkward focus on them, where we end up is effortless brilliance instead of just effortlessly OK. Knowing this process shows us why it's hard, but it also shows us why it's rewarding once you come out the other side.

Through the rest of this book, if you're getting stuck on making some of the changes you want to see, ask yourself where your current skill or habit fits on the scale of unconscious incompetence through to unconscious competence. Diagnosing this question is a big part of making progress.

I is for Inbox Zero

Think Productive runs a number of workshops on different aspects of personal and team productivity, from how to become a Productivity Ninja and run great meetings, through to email etiquette and team collaborations. But the workshop that sells more than any other is all about tackling the email inbox – it's called 'Getting Your Inbox to Zero'.

The term 'inbox zero' was first coined by a blogger called Merlin Mann, who gave a talk on the subject at Google as well as writing about email habits on his blog, 43folders.com. The video of that talk at Google went viral, and over the last few years productivity enthusiasts, app developers and whole organizations have become obsessed with the idea of getting their inboxes to zero. It's not difficult to think about why having zero emails is a compelling thing. For some, it's a daily practice, for others a summit never reached. There has even been a little bit of backlash, from people saying things like: 'Why do I care about getting my inbox to zero anyway?'

In this chapter, I'm going to show you how to get your inbox to zero, and how to keep it there. And then I'll talk about why this matters – after all, email is not your job, it's a *medium* through which the real stuff happens.

The real goal of inbox zero

In the workshops that we run at Think Productive, we see the effect that getting your inbox to zero – usually for the first time since day one in the job – can have on people. Their shoulders relax, they have more of a smile on their face and there's a visible sense of relief, of calm, of having achieved something. It can be truly euphoric when people first see white space and an infinite nothing where they used to see a huge mountain of unwanted rubbish and inarticulate demands.

But while it's truly satisfying to reach 'the end' of email (even if it's only temporarily 'the end' until someone sends you another email), reaching 'the end' is not what makes inbox zero a powerful mindset and habit.

The real reason to get your inbox to zero is to free your mind from thinking about email and to spend less time in your email inbox. Reaching zero emails regularly eliminates distraction, reduces stress and helps clarify what tasks you might still have left to do. Because even when you reach inbox zero, there's still work to do – in fact, it's where the real work begins. There are still conversations to have, ideas to mull, problems to solve and politics to navigate. It's just that when your inbox is at zero, you can see these things more clearly as you'll have sorted out in your own mind or on your to-do list what the result of that mountain of emails actually amounts to in the real world. It's no longer a huge source of discomfort and distraction. It even means you can turn your Outlook or Gmail or Mail app off for a while and do something else.

I don't write with my email inbox turned on in the background. Sometimes I will try even though I know it's a bad idea and end up having a bad productivity day as a result (we're all human!). Deep down, we all know that email is a tool where latest and loudest always trumps the most vital.

THINK ABOUT IT Think about how many times today or this week you've been interrupted from what you were doing by a new email landing in your inbox or a notification on your phone. Out of those times, how many were the most important piece of information you received that day? You get the idea.

So the real purpose of inbox zero isn't to experience a sense of completion (though that is a bonus), it's the *clarity* and *perspective* that the completion brings. Because no-one likes to see a huge pile of things that you think *might* be important, especially not if you know they're on top of another huge pile of things that also might be important but that you can't even see! So, when you have an inbox off the scale and you don't feel good about it, each email needs to follow that CORD process we mentioned earlier. What are the actions worth doing? What are the things that just need to be read quickly and then filed away for future reference or parked as good ideas? What are the emails that need to be deleted?

 Most people I've worked with are shy when it comes to the delete button. We have become a nation of email hoarders, saving up old emails like old ladies who save up used food packets in case they're useful one day. But all those emails are is more distraction, more stress and more weight on your mind that you just don't need.

How to get your inbox to zero

I could go on about this for hours and walk you through every minute step of getting your inbox down to zero, but for the purposes of this short book, I'm going to give you a very quick guide to cutting through your inbox and shedding those emails.

There are three elements to any email inbox:

1. The place where emails land and wait to be managed

2. The place where you continue to manage those emails to which there's some kind of action attached

3. The place where you keep emails that you might need again some other time, but that you don't need now.

The root cause of a lot of stress on email is the fact that people have unclear boundaries in their own minds about where these three places are. Perhaps you have a folder that's for new stuff from your boss but also old stuff from your boss too – so how do you know which of those things you need to look at when you next have time to get some work done?

Most people also have a big pile of emails in their inbox that are a mixture of all three: some new arrivals, some things that need an action or reply *and* some things that they've read and either need to keep or throw away. This syndrome of keeping it all in the inbox is especially true of Gmail users, because Google's search function is so good that you learn to just casually search for the stuff you need, when you need it. Which is fine if you're happy to be generally searching for emails because someone's reminding you that you've missed something! That said, the 'labels' function in Gmail can help solve this issue by effectively acting as the 'containers' or boundaries you need for your emails. If you're a user of one of the more traditional-looking email programs like Outlook, Lotus or Apple Mail, you can use folders to do the same thing.

So, time for clear boundaries.

The inbox

The inbox is just where emails land. They wait in line to be read, replied to, filed away or deleted. In fact, making friends with the delete button is one of the most important things you can do as you set yourself on the way to regular inbox zero.

The first thing you need to do it set up three processing folders. The processing folders are where emails that require some further attention will live. I use:

- **Action** – anything that I need to reply to that takes longer than a few minutes. (If it only takes a few minutes I do it straight away. Remember the two-minute rule?)

- **Read** – chunky long emails that are full of useful or semi-useful news or information, but don't require action. Separating your reading material from your action items is a great way to skim read and batch process all of your reading in one go.

- **Waiting** – anything where I'm waiting on someone else to take action. I can also keep emails here that I've sent to someone else if I'm waiting on their reply and want to remind myself later.

 Using an @ symbol on the names of these folders will make them go to the top of the list in most email programs. So, my folders are called @Action, @Read and @Waiting.

Fourth processing folders?

Perhaps you're thinking that your job requires an extra processing folder? That's fine too. Not everyone needs this one, but I also have a fourth one called '@Diary'. I hate scheduling appointments and find it easier to do several of these in one go, once a day, rather than constantly having to check back to my calendar and remind myself what I'm doing. So if I get an email saying 'can you make this date?' or 'interesting thing happening next Thursday', I batch these up for a day or two and then do them all at the same time. Other examples of additional processing folders are having one called '@Invoices' if you want to store up invoices to pay later, '@Eventname' if you're managing an event and it helps you to have a temporary extra folder to manage the stuff you're working on for that event, and so on. Be careful not to have too many though, and be careful with anything that creates even the slightest uncertainty in your mind as to which folder to use. If you find yourself pausing for a second to think which processing folder to use, then it's usually time to think about merging some folders together.

The library

Below the processing folders is 'the library': all those emails that you want to keep for future reference because they might be useful. Perhaps they're evidence that you did the right thing, perhaps they have useful reminders of key activities or perhaps they just give you a warm glow. The main thing is that they're out of sight and out of mind for now, so you can concentrate more on actions.

There's no hard and fast rule about how many folders to have, but there's one almost-universal truth: very few people have a set of folders they're truly happy with. This is usually for one of two reasons – either you have too many folders and sub-folders or you have a half-thought-out system of folders that isn't clear to you and therefore makes you inclined to leave stuff in the inbox or lose it in the wrong folder.

My suggestion would be not to have more folders than can fit on the screen without scrolling up and down. For most people using Outlook or similar programs, that means about twelve library folders (depending on the size of your screen and what else is in that left-hand column).

You see, the trick is to create an email inbox set-up that makes *filing* easier, not one that you think makes *finding* easier. That's the single biggest reason people have hundreds of unnecessary folders – they think they'll lose everything if it's all in a few big folders rather than in lots of little ones. But think about it: if you had to throw a ball into a bucket, would you rather the bucket was big or small? With fewer folders to check (and with the search box, plus options to sort by date, person and subject at your disposal), it's rare that anything should *ever* be lost in your folders anyway! And besides, filing is something you'll do every time you're looking at emails, whereas searching for old emails is something most of us only do once or twice a week.

Hacking

OK, so you've set up good processing folders and library folders (or labels if you're a Gmail user). Now it's time to do the initial clear-out down to zero. How long should this take? Well, if you follow these instructions, my experience (from delivering hundreds of workshops doing exactly this) is that it should take no longer than three hours.

Hacking is about clearing out the dead wood in your inbox. And you have more of it than you think. With email – especially email that's older than a few days – use the 800/20 rule. For every 800 emails you have in your inbox, only twenty will actually require attention and action. The trick and purpose of hacking is to get to those twenty as quickly as you can. To do this, you need to look for opportunities to deal with more than one email at a time – groups of ten, twenty, fifty or even several hundred – all filed, deleted or moved out of your inbox with clarity and purpose in just one keystroke or mouse click.

Hacking: email death row

The first and biggest hack is to sort everything by date. Then, pick a cut-off date. Most people use somewhere around six months ago, but some will say three months or even sooner. Everything before that date you're going to move to a folder called 'email death row'. Then, in the coming weeks, you can start to see if you needed anything from that folder at all. In a few weeks' time when you're confident you've rescued anything of value, you can delete the rest. In one go. This is powerful because it changes your relationship with those emails from 'I'm sure there's important stuff in there somewhere …' to 'I'm actively side-lining those emails and waiting to see if there was anything important in there.' Much more proactive. Cheating? Some might say that. I'd simply say that when you have several thousand emails and you need to get to what matters, you need all the help you can get! Cheating, when it comes to email, is part of the game.

Hacking: go for the big wins
Hacking means looking at your emails differently and find-ing ways to make one decision about multiple emails in one go. Naturally, as you start to hack, you should be presented with big opportunities ('death row' is probably the biggest and easiest to start with), and then the more you hack, the smaller the groups of emails you will find. Hacking ends when you're left with a pile of 'individual' emails, where no grouping will make it easier.

When you're hacking, the trick is to avoid getting drawn into the detailed text of any emails. If something is starting to draw your attention, skip it and move on. Look for the stuff that you can chop or file in bulk without much of a sec-ond thought. Develop some momentum, become friendlier with the delete button, chuck whole groups of emails into folders and keep moving quickly. The best way to keep the momentum going is to regularly change the view on your screen. I would suggest this order in general, but it's good to flit between the views just to keep it fresh:

- Date – for 'email death row' only

- From – to clear out all those unnecessary marketing emails or ones from people who you don't work with anymore

- Subject – look for the conversations, out of offices and irrelevant banter.

Then keep flitting between 'from' and 'subject', this time probably looking for slightly smaller groups, if you did your initial hacking job properly.

Processing

You'll know instinctively when hacking is over. You'll probably feel mentally tired after deleting or filing so many emails, maybe going back several months or even years. When you're left with a pile that you need to go through one by one, mainly consisting of recent or important emails, you know you're ready to move into processing mode.

The diagram on page 83 details the thought process to develop really disciplined email processing. Apply this by taking each email in turn. Don't skip around and don't procrastinate when one email is hard. Start at the bottom and work your way to the top. It might be that each email here takes much longer than when you were hacking. That's natural. And you'll probably start to find that you use the processing folders much more, the delete button a bit less and maybe the library folders a bit less too. But you're on the home straight to inbox zero here. It's less satisfying than bludgeoning 100 old emails in one fell swoop, but it's just as important.

Zero

When you reach zero, take a moment to look around. There's nothing new waiting for a decision. Nothing.

However, in the @Action folder there will probably be some emails that still need some love and attention. I tend to think that if I have twenty or so in this folder, that's about right. I will regularly try and clear it out (even down to zero), but equally if I'm not spending too much time there, it may creep up to 40 or 50. I always know that over 50 means I need to give my @Action folder some serious attention. You will probably find that similar guiding numbers work for you, but this is very much a personal thing. The key is whether you feel it tugging on your attention when you're trying to get something else done.

Take a moment to settle into this new way of thinking about your email inbox. I promise you, when you first get to zero, it can change your whole attitude to email, and even to information in general. Once you've got there it's a habit that's easy to make permanent, since on any given day

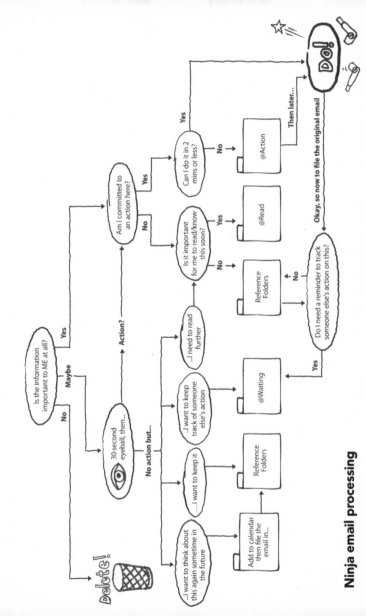

Ninja email processing

you're only dealing with that day or that week, not the big pile of stuff from months ago! Email processing can easily be something that's done in less than an hour a day once you have good systems and habits in place.

Turning email off

What's also empowering is the ability to turn email off without feeling guilty. If you're clear on what needs to be done, you can be clear on how important any of it is. And with this in mind, you'll know when it's possible to live life outside of your email inbox.

 Sometime this week sit at your desk for a couple of hours with your email program turned off. It's interesting to observe how, if you're not used to this, you will initially spend a lot of time 'grasping' for your inbox! But once you get used to it being turned off, you'll be amazed at the focus and clarity that you're able to devote to other tasks without the constant awareness that it's there in the background waiting to ping.

When NOT to bother with inbox zero

I started this chapter by saying that there has been a small backlash against the very idea of inbox zero, and there may be some circumstances when the time it takes to maintain a zero inbox outweighs the benefit. For example, I have a personal email account that I never get to zero. I only use it for signing up to new software or air tickets or booking websites. I use it so that when devious companies sell my data and I start receiving lots of unwanted marketing, it goes somewhere else and not to my main inbox. And I don't care about whether it's a zero because there's nothing in that inbox that I need to keep on top of, or keep track of. If I need to find something in there, I can just search for it.

Likewise, if your role means that your mission-critical work happens away from your inbox, and you're not at all scared, stressed or concerned about missing something coming in via email, then you don't need to keep your inbox at zero. I know a few chief executives who rely on their assistant to flag up anything urgent, and they are so mentally attuned to piecemeal working (where their interests or subject areas are vast yet their involvement shallow) that they don't feel the need to manage email that tightly. So email piles up, but it's not a source of stress. In that instance, it may make sense not to bother with attempting inbox zero.

But if you're occasionally stressed by the contents of your email, it helps to have a way to stop emails falling through the cracks and getting missed. Or if you want to develop a way to spend less time in your inbox and have more of your attention left to focus on the stuff that matters, then inbox zero is not only the best strategy out there, it's much more achievable than you might think.

J is for Juice

In primary school I was fond of telling really bad jokes. One of my favourites was this:

Q: Why did the orange stop rolling down the hill?
A: Because it ran out of juice.

What we need to make things happen these days isn't just time, but attention. In particular, we need as much of our best attention – our proactive attention – as possible, and at the right times. But what if attention were different to time? What if it were truly possible that, rather than simply managing your precious and scarce attention, you could actually create *more* proactive attention?

One productivity topic that is often overlooked is how we manage our bodies and brains. This is a vast subject area, of course, worthy of several books in and of itself (and there are plenty out there). From what we eat and drink to how we move, how we sit and how we sleep, there are a lot of possible reasons why we feel energized one day but lethargic the next.

So where do you get your 'juice', and how do you stop running out of it? Are there things that you do that you know make you feel better? Personally, I know a short run first thing in the morning warms up my body and tends to put my brain into a fuller state of concentration. This is particularly true if I feel tired when I wake. I also know that if

I'm delivering a workshop or likely to be on my feet all day, then porridge is the only breakfast that gets me through until lunch without me feeling hungry and fidgety. I know that 'superfoods' and certain vitamins help me to avoid that end of day 'zone-out' and prolong the length of time later in the day that I feel fully alert. And I know that while I'm lucky enough to be able to have a few beers or glasses of wine without getting a headache the next day, I *will* feel lethargic and spaced out.

There is a whole plethora of ways to look after your body and mind, some of which will have a more noticeable effect on your attention and energy than others. It's a topic that cries out for extra attention if you're serious about creating the impact in the world that extra energy and proactive attention can give you. For now, here are a few quick things to illustrate how looking after your health and well-being in order to improve your energy and productivity doesn't need to be a huge extra commitment.

Ten quick tips to give you more juice

1. Combine exercise with something else instead of going to the gym

The psychological effect of adding the gym as yet another chore or another thing to maintain in your already busy life means it's destined to result in disappointment. Instead, think about what you already do that you could do differently. Rather than walking the dog, try running with the dog. Cycle or run to work, or if you have five minutes to wait for a train or bus, spend that five minutes walking up and down the platform or stairs. There are plenty of ways to tweak your existing commitments rather than adding in a new one.

2. Make your own microwave meals and freezer supplies

The supermarket's microwave meals are usually full of salt and fat, but if you're making a curry, it's just as easy to make six portions as is it to make two. So, buy a few plastic container boxes and make your own healthy microwave meals! Similarly, one of the hassles and time barriers to cooking with fresh ingredients is all the chopping and preparation. So, for items that you chop and use regularly such as onions, chillies and peppers, buy these in bulk, chop them in bulk, and then you have a ready-made stash of them in your freezer for weeks to come. (This tip saves lots of money too!) You'll not only be eating more healthily, but on days when you're absolutely shattered from work, you'll know that you don't have to come home and cook.

3. Keep vitamins in every location

Instead of buying one pot of multivitamins and always forgetting to take them, keep a pot in your desk at work, a pot at home (preferably next to whatever you have for breakfast) and another one in your bag. That way, you've always got a backup and are less likely to forget it.

4. Start as you mean to go on

If you're struggling with instilling a particular habit, try starting the day by solving it; you'll get yourself into the swing of it. For me, this means drinking a pint of water early in the morning. I know that doing this makes it more likely I'll keep drinking water all day long.

5. Make it so small it feels like cheating

With exercise and healthy eating, even a small amount will be good for you, and, crucially, it will mean that you make a habit of succeeding, not failing. For example, even a five-minute brisk run first thing in the morning will boost your metabolism and make you feel great. It doesn't need to take half an hour! And eating one piece of fruit rather than worrying about your 'five a day' will encourage you to get onto the rest of them.

6. Meditate on the bus

In the Z is for Zen chapter, we will look at meditation, which is another brilliant tool for increasing proactive attention. Many people feel they don't have time to meditate or don't know where to start, yet it's something you can do easily on the bus or train to or from work. There are even apps for your phone, such as Buddhify and Headspace, which have specific guided meditations for when you're on the move. So, just put your headphones in and follow the instructions.

7. Learn good floor exercises and do them in front of the TV

Exercising and strengthening key muscle groups can feel daunting, but you don't need a gym full of weights to get the right exercise. A quick look online will give you a full range of videos, and from there you can develop a routine that you can follow at home, even combining it with your favourite TV show. Personally, I like to do planks and sit-ups at home and have some simple dumbbell weights too.

8. Walk or run the last bit home

If you commute to work, get off the bus or the Tube and walk or run that last bit home. Or, if you need to get something from the shops, choose the second nearest instead of the nearest one. Make it a fun way to add an extra five minutes onto something you were doing already and it won't feel so painful.

9. Keep healthy snacks in your bag to stop you needing to buy chocolate

When you get those midday hunger pangs, it's easy to reach for a chocolate bar or a slice of that cake from the office bake-off competition. But if you have healthy alternatives nearby, you're more likely to resist. Keep granola bars, nuts, dried fruit and apples in your bag or desk so that when you find yourself reaching for a snack, healthy eating is the easiest thing, not a chore or some kind of distant new year's resolution.

10. Swap coffee for apples

Crashing after caffeine is a sure-fire way to drain your attention. Use coffee strategically, but substitute some of those coffees for apples or water instead. Apples are full of natural sugars, so they give you the same high as the coffee, just without such a crash afterwards.

Actual juice

Most of the things your parents and teachers told you about health when you were growing up are true: we should all eat more fruit and vegetables, eat less junk food, get plenty of exercise, drink more water and breathe more fresh air. Common sense isn't always commonly practised. One of my favourite productivity boosters is to make my own healthy juices and smoothies. The great thing about doing it myself is I know exactly what goes into them, and, especially first thing in the morning, this can be a great way to kick-start my day by kick-starting my metabolism.

Here are a couple of my favourite juice and smoothie recipes. Why not experiment and make your own?

Beetroot and apple smoothie

This is a nice simple one. Beetroot is fantastic brain food: according to a study at Wake Forest University, it is full of nitrates, which increase blood flow to the brain and improve mental performance. At the same time, it's a natural way to reduce your blood pressure and feel calmer in your work.

Ingredients:

- Two beetroots (a.k.a. beets). You can do this raw, but I prefer to use cooked.

- One large or two small apples

- Half a cucumber

- The juice from half a lemon

- Water or ice cubes

You can also add in coconut water, garlic, light greens like kale or spinach, ginger or anything else you fancy.

This should make two portions, but you can always double up and leave enough for tomorrow. (Although it's worth noting that any longer than a day and you start to lose the freshness of the ingredients, so quadrupling the recipe isn't advisable.)

Simple green juice

Green vegetables like spinach and kale are full of iron and tend to be great ways to get a full range of vitamins and antioxidants, too. What's also great for the lazy and busy among us is that you can buy frozen spinach from the supermarket, so that you never run out – a couple of minutes soaking in water while you prepare the rest of the ingredients and you're good to go. Again, this makes two servings.

Ingredients:

- Two large handfuls of fresh spinach or kale

- Half a cucumber

- Half a small pineapple (chopped)

- One mango (chopped)

- One banana

- Water or ice cubes

As with all of these drinks, you can add in anything else you fancy: apples, cucumber, ginger … and whatever else is going bad in your refrigerator!

 It's annoying to know that so much of that obnoxious and nagging health advice is actually really important – believe me, I'd love to be able to get all my nutritional needs from beer and chocolate! – but taking your health seriously and understanding what your body and brain need to function well is a vital component of productivity. There are, of course, people who take health and fitness to an extreme and allow it to become the sole focus in their lives, but hopefully you're seeing from this chapter that there are some simple and practical changes you can make that don't actually need to take over your life to make a difference to your productivity!

K is for Kitchen Timers and Keyboard Shortcuts

Kitchen timers

What has a kitchen timer got to do with productivity? Well, Francesco Cirillo's famous productivity book, *The Pomodoro Technique*, is all about using a kitchen timer to manage your attention, working in 'sprints' that count down from 25 minutes to zero, followed by a five minute break. ('Pomodoro' is the Italian word for 'tomato', and I think we all remember those old tomato-shaped kitchen timers.) The idea is that during each 'pomodoro', you screen out procrastination and distractions by knowing that you have a five-minute break coming up, and that by stopping after 25 minutes you are able to maintain a more balanced flow of energy throughout the day. It's a particularly great technique for people who easily fall prey to distractions. You can find out more at pomodorotechnique.com.

 Think about a task you have coming up that's going to take an hour or more. Break the task down into 25-minute dashes (pomodoros). How many pomodoros do you think you'll need to complete the activity? Use this strategy to measure the activity as you go, too; it's a great way to develop your awareness of how long things actually take and how you use your own time and attention.

Keyboard shortcuts

As easy and intuitive as the mouse is to use, it's far quicker if you can master keyboard shortcuts for tasks that you do regularly. Use keyboard shortcuts to perform regular commands, such as launching a new program, starting a new email or editing text in a document.

There are basic keyboard shortcuts that almost everyone uses, and then there's a whole range of others that you might not know about. It's worth spending a bit of time familiarizing yourself with the best shortcuts for your computer and the programs you use most, as once you've mastered them they can be a great time-saver. You can find a great general list of up-to-date PC and Mac shortcuts at www.shortcutworld.com, and if you use a particular piece of software regularly (whether it be Microsoft Word, Google Chrome, Apple Keynote or something much more obscure), you will usually find that a 5-minute web search will throw up some really useful shortcuts you never knew existed.

 Think of a piece of software you use regularly, find a few keyboard shortcuts you don't currently use and try them out a few times. You'll be surprised at how easily you can incorporate them into your working life. A top tip here is to print out five new ones and pin them next to your computer until you've learned them – then print out five more!

L is for Lists

It's time to talk about your to-do list. Have you ever made a to-do list when you felt stressed and by the end of writing the list, you felt better? Have you ever been sat staring at a to-do list so long you found yourself needing to re-write it and add to it before you were ready to actually do any work? Both of these things are good indicators of our real relationship with the humble to-do list.

We use a to-do list to remind us of what needs to be done and to keep us orientated in our work so that we make good priority decisions. When you feel stressed and you reach for the pen and paper, it's a good sign that keeping all of those ideas and commitments in your head is bad for you – there's no bigger distraction when you're trying to do something important than the panicked thought of something that's unimportant. So, as you manage more complexity and a wider range of projects and actions than ever before, keeping everything on a to-do list is no longer a luxury. Managing your lists in the right way is one of the key habits of not only being productive but staying sane!

If you find yourself rewriting the list and rethinking the things on there, it's an indication that you no longer trust your to-do list to do its job of keeping you orientated. The most common problem is having more things to do that you haven't yet written on the list; so you're trying to work out whether the things on the list or the things still in your brain are what's most important. In fact, your brain itself is great at making decisions but pretty awful at holding more than a few things in your short-term memory at once or knowing in which order to do things without getting stressed.

So, treat your to-do list as a 'second brain': a place that takes care of the memory aspects of your tasks, leaving you to focus on the prioritizing and execution. To do its job properly, you may need that second brain to be a little bit more complex than a simple list on the back of an envelope. In this chapter, I'm going to share with you the 'architecture' of lists I use. (Conveniently, they're also the same lists used in the CORD Productivity Model we discussed earlier.)

The key components of your second brain

Most people like to have a list of the things they're doing that day, but the bit that's often missing is how this relates to the wider context of what you're working on at that time – the ongoing projects you're involved in and the stuff that you still want to do but won't get around to doing today. So, design your second brain in a way to bring all of these elements together, usually in one place, to make it a whole lot easier. Let's first of all paint a picture of the main components:

- Projects List
- Master Actions List
- Daily To-do List.

Projects List

This is a simple list of all the projects you're working on. Anything that you'll still be doing next week or that requires more than a couple of actions should be considered as a project, so you don't forget about it. In my experience, while many people have a team work plan, they don't have an individual list of the projects they're working on. To give some examples, 'completing the appraisal process for my team', 'agreeing new rental arrangements for the office' and 'being best man at Nathan's wedding' are all examples of projects. (Likewise, until you know exactly the holiday you want to book, the dates you want to go and the company that you'll book it with, 'book holiday' is probably a project, not an action!). On this list you don't need to go into lots of detail *about* the projects. The idea is simply so that when you come to review your lists and think about the next actions for each project, you have a complete list of the projects you need to put your attention to.

Master Actions List

Your Master Actions List should be a complete list of everything you could possibly be doing today. That's not to say you'll do it all today, but at any given time it's important to know what your options could be. You probably find that this list gets LONG, as it should contain at least one action item from every single project on your Projects List, so you'll need to break it up. The best way to break it up is to divide it into the places where the work happens. You might have several places, such as:

- Office

- Home

- Out and about (such as buying stationery or delivering things to a client)

- In the team meeting.

Dividing this list by location allows you to focus straight in on what needs to happen in the office when you're in the office, focus only on your working-from-home activities when you're working from home, and so on. It means you're always prepared for wherever you are. It also allows you to do really clever things like have a 'thinking' list or an 'anywhere' list, so that when you're sat there feeling bored on a delayed train, you can call up that list on your phone or in your notebook and have something really productive that you can do. You never know when the opportunity might arise, so being prepared pays dividends. Likewise, this means that when you're in the office you don't have a huge list to look through; you're totally focused on those activities that need you to be in the office to do.

Daily To-do List
Finally, at the start of the day (or the night before), you will probably want to make a Daily To-do List to focus in on the

things that are most important for that day. Use the Master Actions List to review all of your options. If you were relying on a new Daily To-do List alone and didn't have the benefit of these other lists and extra layers of structure, you'd be relying on your own brain to remember all the most crucial things. It can be a big cause of stress trying to juggle all of those commitments inside your brain, so getting it all down on paper means you have clarity and calm in which to make your prioritization decisions and can be fully confident that you're making great choices. If at the end of the day you don't quite get through the full Daily To-do List, you know that the information is all still sat within the Master Actions List for you to come back to afresh tomorrow.

What other lists do I need in my second brain?

There are two other very useful lists to keep. Again, both are key components of the CORD Productivity Model. These two are for when you know there's not an action for you to be doing next, but there's some information, actions or ideas that you want to keep track of somehow. These are:

- Waiting For List

- Good Ideas Park.

Waiting For List

One of the biggest problems with personal productivity is that it's, well, personal! What happens when you keep track of everything and do an amazing job of managing all your projects and actions, yet everyone around you is letting the side down? Well, you keep track of what you need *them* to do, too! So the Waiting For List is where you track those things that other people are committed to achieving that matter to projects you're working on. For example, I have been working with a graphic designer to design a new marketing brochure. I've come up with my ideas, we've had a meeting to discuss the brief, and the designer is coming back to me next Friday. At the same time, the designer also mentioned a cool new website he wanted me to have a look at, but he hasn't sent me the link yet. So, there I have two little actions that my designer has committed to. These sit on my Waiting For List, so that I remember to chase them up. If I wasn't that bothered about the cool new website the designer mentioned, there's no need to write it down – if it happens, it happens. The criteria for what goes on this list are simple: what do you care about enough to keep track of? If you're using an app, this can sit easily within the rest of the Master Actions List, but obviously you'll still need to treat it differently, as your only job here is to track and occasionally chase up.

Good Ideas Park

It's tempting when you have a great new idea to turn it straight into a project or action – then suddenly you feel committed to it until it's done. However, things change with time. When you had the idea you might have already been thinking about how to get it done, yet a few days later you might start thinking that actually you've got bigger priorities right now. Likewise, you might have an idea that you just know will come in really handy in six months' time, but right now is just not the right time for it. If you keep a list of these things separately to your Master Actions List and Projects List, in your mind it allows you to consciously 'un-commit' from making those ideas happen right now. You put a barrier between the things you're working on and need to put your attention to, and those things which would be nice to work on, but not necessarily right now. And of course, as time rolls on, some of those things in the Good Ideas Park become brilliant ideas and turn into projects and actions, while others stay on the shelf, and others still wither away and are eventually deleted.

Setting up your lists

So, there you have it: the five lists that comprise your second brain. It's a bit more complicated than just writing a to-do list on the back of an old piece of paper – and it might take you a few days or even weeks to get fully used to it – but that's the difference between something that works and something that doesn't. So, if you feel like you've kept to-do lists but they've never stopped you from feeling stressed, or that you need a bit more clarity and control in your working world, then keeping an up-to-date second brain will do exactly that. We will focus later on the habit of reviewing your second brain weekly and daily (as part of the 'Weekly Checklist' chapter), which will help you with the challenge of making these new habits and approaches actually stick.

Two key questions to finish this chapter:

1. Thinking about your current habits, which of these lists are you already keeping and using in some form or another? What new ideas here do you see that might help you?

2. In terms of where to keep your lists, there are lots of options (and there's much more detail on this in the 'Tools' chapter), but for now, what are you currently using, and what do you think might benefit you out of the following options?
   (a) A web-based or smartphone to-do list app
   (b) Something familiar like Microsoft Word, Excel or Outlook Tasks
   (c) Good old-fashioned pen and paper.

None of these is right or wrong – the trick here is to use something that you're comfortable with (more of which in the 'Tools' chapter).

M is for Meetings

The Attention Tension

When we fully grasp the idea of proactive attention – the idea that for a small amount of time each day our attention and energy puts us on top form – then two things are clear. Firstly, we need to be as agile and nimble in how we schedule our work as our job role will allow us to be. Secondly, it is productivity suicide to waste those precious few hours of proactive attention sat in someone else's boring meeting.

Nobody really likes meetings. They elicit a similar groan to PowerPoint presentations and networking. Yet, just like PowerPoint presentations and networking, what we're really down on is not the medium or method itself but the astonishingly bad usage of them by so many people. A great PowerPoint presentation or a great piece of networking can be truly inspiring and really productive. So can a great meeting.

A great meeting often highlights how a team working well together can bring an outcome greater than the sum of its parts. It highlights the interdependency that is arguably a greater feature of work now than it has ever been. Yet, by definition, that also creates an obligation to attend and contribute to meetings that perhaps are not your biggest priority. Herein lies the paradox of meetings. We need to reduce their frequency, often reduce their length and certainly increase their impact, but we also need good meetings to make the world go round, just as much as we need to claw back the attention we lose by sitting in some of the bad ones. I call this contradiction the 'Attention Tension'.

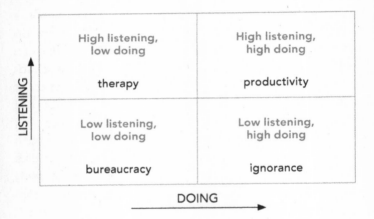

Riding the thin line between listening and doing is something each of us needs to think about deeply, both as individuals and in our teams and organizations.

To start to do this, here are three pieces of action you can take:

1. **Calculate your 'cost of meeting'.** If you add up the hourly rates of everyone in the room, plus the costs of maintaining said room, it can quickly become clear that some meetings are literally a waste of time and money. Learning to view meetings and people's attention as a

finite resource, no different from (and indeed intrinsically linked to) your departmental budget, can help to make the connection between input and outcome.

2. **Develop a culture of really smart, action-orientated meetings,** so that when you do meet, you're respecting everyone's time and attention fully. Even in organizations with terrible meetings cultures, you can swim against the tide and be a role model for the change that *will* start to occur once everyone sees the benefit.

3. **Individually and as a company, develop the habit of listening.** It's important to listen beyond the words and be mindful of the other dynamics at play, such as ego, pay grade and departmental expertise. Often the most important idea doesn't come from the loudest or most obvious person.

Meetings and the 40-20-40 continuum

At Think Productive, we are lucky to work with international facilitator Martin Farrell, who facilitates meetings large and small for organizations including the UN Climate Change Secretariat, the Fairtrade Foundation and the European Commission. Martin also worked on the book *Meeting Together* with Lois Graessle and George Gawlinski. In it, they introduce the 40-20-40 continuum, a model for thinking about the focus and effort that meetings require.

The theory is this: focus 40 per cent of your attention for each meeting on preparation and getting everything right before you meet, 20 per cent of your attention on the meeting itself – the time you're all together – and then 40 per cent of your attention on the follow-through.

Like all golden rules, it appears to be simple and even a little obvious on first view, but in applying it, you start to see that the way we structure our effort around meetings is so biased towards that middle 20 per cent. Yet it's often the 40 per cent at the beginning that shapes the entire success or failure of a meeting. Crucial to the meeting having any impact is, of course, following up to ensure that things actually happen afterwards.

What I find particularly useful and inspiring about the 40-20-40 continuum is that it gives permission before a meeting to prepare in a way that means your meeting will get results, rather than regarding preparation as unnecessary labour. You can also use the model during a meeting to alert participants to the importance of follow-through. By doing this, you can make sure that the end of the meeting is framed as a beginning: because it introduces the follow-through phase by summarizing and organizing the action points from a meeting.

Here are a few tips based around this 40-20-40 principle that I hope will help you question the need for certain meetings and transform the meetings you have.

40 per cent before

Purpose. Are you *and* all other attendees clear on what the intended outcome of the meeting should be and how you'll know if you've achieved it? Make sure your agenda includes a simple statement of purpose: 'By the end of this meeting we will ...'

Practicalities. Does it need to be a 'physical' meeting at all? Would Skype, phone, webinar or something else be a better option? Are we presuming it should be an hour long because that's what we've always done? What would it look like if we changed it to fifteen minutes?

Place. The room, the cakes, the comfort level: these things matter if you're serious about giving people an environment in which to think, appreciate, contribute and decide. Great creative and strategic decisions are rarely made in dimly-lit basements!

Pace. You can only go as fast as the slowest person in the room, so what can you do by way of preparation to get people up to speed and ready to fully participate? Use the meeting itself for discussion and decision, not information-sharing that can be done more productively by people in their own time.

Plan. Ever thought about writing the minutes of a meeting BEFORE the meeting happens? Of course things will change on the day, but doing this will give you the time to fully prepare and anticipate the consequences or nuances of the discussion. It will also help to give you a clearer idea about what a successful outcome might look like.

20 per cent during

Participation. Create an environment where people's contributions are valued. Meetings where only the loudest are heard don't suit everyone's learning style, and sometimes the quietest of contributions are the ones you most need to hear.

Pace and pauses. Try to take a step back from the discussions to notice body language and be conscious of whether people's attention or enthusiasm may be flagging. Remember, no matter how fascinating the discussion, it's never as memorable or attention-grabbing as a full bladder!

Practicalities. Ensure that you or one of your team looks after the practicalities so that you leave participants to focus on the thinking, learning or decision making.

40 per cent after

Productive follow-through. There's no point everyone signing up to actions or committing to further work if none of those people is going to be held accountable after the meeting has ended. Ensure during the meeting that every action has a single owner and a clear deadline. During the meeting, talk about how and when people will be held accountable and when progress will be reviewed. Follow up quickly after the meeting to confirm the details of who's doing what – the day after a meeting is the crucial time to either capitalize on the momentum gained or lose it completely.

N is for Ninja

In 2012, after spending five years or so working with organizations and individuals to help them create the impact they wanted and tackle the problems of stress and information overload, I wrote and released the first version of my book, *How to be a Productivity Ninja*. Writing it was a really useful process in working out what I knew about productivity. One of the things that started to become clear to me was that, as much as you can dictate or suggest particular models or methods that undoubtedly help to improve your productivity, what's more important is to develop the mindset to help you make great productivity decisions and adapt to new situations.

When the enemy is information overload, stress, tiredness, having too much to do and feeling overwhelmed by the requests and expectations of others, do you want to surrender and be a victim? Or do you want to be a Productivity Ninja?

Adopting the approach and mentality of a Ninja can work wonders for your productivity. In such a short book and with such a plethora of other things to cover, we can't go into huge levels of detail here, but here in this chapter is 'the way of the Productivity Ninja': the nine key characteristics of the Productivity Ninja.

1. Zen-like Calm

Great decision making comes from creating the time and space to think rationally and intelligently about the issue at hand. Decisions made during periods of panic are likely to be the ones we want to forget about. The Ninja realizes this, remains calm in the face of adversity and equally calm under the pressure of information overload. You might not believe this, but it is entirely possible to have 101 things still to do and remain absolutely calm. So, how do we beat stress and remain calm?

Be sure that you're not distracted and stressed by what you *could* be forgetting by using a second brain instead of your own head as the place where information and reminders live. This is certainly easier said than done, but once mastered, it really works.

2. Ruthlessness

As well as needing to make more and better decisions, we need to be choosier, too, processing information to sort the wheat from the chaff, see the timber from the trees, and sorting the big opportunities from the even bigger ones. Ruthlessness isn't just about how we process information though; it's also about our ability to protect our time and attention, focusing only on the things that add the greatest impact, even at the expense of other things that are 'worth doing'.

Being ruthless also means being selective about how we achieve our goals. In some areas of our work, perfection is healthy and even necessary, but in other cases, it needs to be avoided as it prevents us from moving on to the next thing and isn't efficient.

3. Weapon-savvy

The Ninja is skilful on their own but knows that using the right tools makes them more effective. There are a range of tools out there to help keep us on top of our game. There are two broad types of tools that the Productivity Ninja needs to have in their armoury:

- **Thinking tools**, such as checklists and management models, provide a way to guide our thinking through tried and tested themes and questions. Because they're models, they don't rely on our own memory, so they work just as well at 4pm on a Friday as at 10am on a Monday.

- **Organizing tools**, such as to-do list software or well-ordered paper systems, give us clarity around what we're doing and help ensure that no project or action gets forgotten at a vital moment.

See the chapter on 'Tools' for more information on specific thinking and organizing tools.

4. Stealth and Camouflage

One of the worst things you can do is make yourself always available. It's an invitation to some of your biggest enemies: distraction and interruption. Keep out of the limelight until you've got something you need others to hear.

If your attention and focus is likely to be impeded by unlimited access to the internet and you're likely to be tempted by its millions of distraction possibilities (and who isn't?), disconnect once in a while. Yes, *turn off* the internet! If I turn off my Wi-Fi connection for two hours, I get two hours of uninterrupted thinking time. How many of your best ideas really came to you when you were sat behind a desk staring at incoming emails?

5. Unorthodoxy

What's important is the end result, not how you get there. Everything else is up for grabs. A Productivity Ninja should recognize that it doesn't matter how the job gets done; the important thing is that it's done. It's important to be on constant lookout for every opportunity to take advantage of progress and innovation and to do things more easily. We must avoid getting stuck in a rut and doing things less efficiently than we could, at all costs.

Doing things differently is risky, even when we've got a good hunch that we've got a better way of doing things. Managers generally prefer the status quo as it gives them an easier life, so doing the thing that challenges the status quo can often tread a fine line between glory and failure. But this isn't about chasing glory (although we'll reluctantly and graciously accept it when it comes along), it's about doing things in a better way and experiencing the satisfaction that comes from pushing boundaries.

6. Agility

A Ninja needs to be light on their feet, able to respond with deftness to new opportunities or threats. Anything that requires a lot of shifting of thinking, quick reactions and decisions will, of course, need our proactive attention. As we know, this is a finite resource. Our ability to react quickly and  appropriately to new challenges really comes down to two things:

- Our own mental reserves and capacity to spend more of our days in a proactive 'doing' mode without getting tired. People do this temporarily through the use of caffeine or other stimulants, which is fine to an extent and in the short term, but we need to think more sustainably than that. (Go back to 'J is for Juice' for more ideas on this.)

- Our ability to bring in other resources to aid this process – other people, more time and better technology.

7. Mindfulness

Our minds are our most important tool. Being emotionally intelligent and self-aware is important for so many reasons, not least because it equips you to take action.

Steven Pressfield's book *The War of Art* is a revealing and personal account of his battles as a writer against what he calls 'the resistance'. The resistance is a mindset characterized by stress, anxiety, fear of failure, fear of success and a whole host of other emotions that whir around our brains and tell us to stand still. Your job as a Ninja is to navigate those thought processes as much as possible, because resistance is the enemy of productivity. Meditation, regular review of your work and designing 'thinking checklists' to guide your intuition are some of the techniques you can use here.

8. Preparedness

Preparedness underpins and strengthens so many of the other characteristics we've just talked about. Zen-like calm in the heat of the battle is only possible if you're well-prepared. Agility is only possible if you're starting from a position of being prepared and ready to react immediately, producing the right response. And you're only ready to be ruthless if you've got the energy. Being prepared is about practical preparation as well as mental preparation. Lunch is not for wimps and rest and renewal is vital for longer-term success.

9. A Ninja is not superhuman ... but they sometimes appear to be

Finally, it's important to note that a Ninja is NOT a superhero. There are too many gurus out there telling you how to be perfect, and in doing so, they're selling you a false dream. Don't listen to them. A Ninja is a human being, with all the foibles and imperfections that we humans have. We can improve, we can do our best and increase productivity to levels that make us seem like we're productivity superheroes, but we're still prone to the odd moment of making the wrong decision or screwing things up. It's time we focused more on the 99 things we do brilliantly than the one we screw up. Imperfection is a reassuring reminder that there's always more to learn.

THINK ABOUT IT So, those are the nine characteristics that make up the Productivity Ninja mindset. Which of those nine characteristics do you think you need to develop to be more like a Productivity Ninja?

O is for Over-promising

Over-promising is a bad thing

One of the hardest things about the work superhero para-digm is that everyone in your team at work wants to look like a superhero and everyone in your team expects you to be a superhero too. As we discussed in the previous chap-ter, a Productivity Ninja may appear to be a superhero, but they're still human. So, when your boss approaches you with a new piece of work and says, 'Do you think you can drop everything and get this done?', or when there's a fire to put out or a complex problem to solve, we all start to invoke those superhero mantras. 'No problem! I'm amazing! To infinity and beyond!'

We even do this with ourselves. Hofstadter's Law states that 'it always takes longer than you expect, even when you take into account Hofstadter's Law'. When you have ambi-tion and want to achieve impact, it's really hard to properly evaluate the time commitments and consequences of what you say yes to – just as it's hard to walk slowly down the road after you've had an exciting piece of news or are stressed about being late for something.

So we need to think about the negative repercussions of over-promising. Overcoming the superhero syndrome and recognizing the human version of you is tough. It's tough for the ego, it's potentially career-damaging if you work in an organization with a terrible aversion to balance, and it's potentially uncomfortable as you explore the foibles and failures that make you uniquely and wonderfully human.

To do this we need to get better at saying no to ourselves and to others. No one enjoys saying no to other people, and it's even harder when you're worried that you might let somebody down (and expose yourself as the normal human being that you are!).

 Here are five ways to help practice your ability to say no:

1. **Use 'Force delete' as a weekly habit** when you review your Master Actions List. Each week, delete three things you had previously committed to. Doing this helps to instil a mindset of constant renegotiation and evolution of the to-do list. There's nothing worse than a to-do list that becomes stagnant with things that weren't vital three weeks ago but are even less vital now.

2. **Stop telling white lies and confront the 'no' head on.** Stop saying, 'I'm busy on that day' and start giving the real reason instead: 'Sorry, I've taken too much on already so don't want to commit to something more', or 'Sorry, this doesn't fulfil one of my priorities right now'. This can be uncomfortable, but practise it. In time you'll become more comfortable with the idea that priorities often compete and you can't be nice and helpful all the time.

3. **Learn to leave meetings without a huge new list of things to do.** Before you attend any meeting, think about the limit of what you can take on – how much time do you have spare to help with the project at hand? If it helps, tell a colleague in the meeting that you plan to commit to less than an hour's worth of follow-up. They could decide to do the same. Then you make it a game so that when the time comes and the meeting seeks volunteers, you stay silent or you say no.

4. **Fight fire with facts.** If your boss is keen to delegate more and more things, use your up-to-date Master Actions List and Projects List to have an objective conversation where you ask them to choose what you can drop or de-prioritize. Most of the time, the 'can you take on more stuff?' conversation is not objective; it's held with the subtext of, 'You're a superhero though, aren't you?', or 'You're just not getting through everything quickly enough, are you?' With the facts to hand rather than just the guilt and judgement, you'll help both of you to have a more informed discussion about your workload.

5. **Get a gatekeeper.** If you have an assistant or another person in the team who has responsibility for your diary or your projects, discuss with them where you need to put your attention and the kinds of things that you regret saying yes to. That way, they can help you by acting as a gatekeeper. If someone else is screening your

emails, they can say no to things on your behalf and also pull you back from the temptation of saying yes when certain requests come in.

Saying no is truly one of the most difficult things to do. Being ruthless with where you put your attention and focus means being ruthless with what you say no to, so that the things that you say yes to truly have your attention. You have to be cruel to be kind.

Over-promising is a good thing (sometimes)

The letter 'O' also starts off 'On the other hand' ... Now let's talk about when over-promising can actually be one of the greatest productivity weapons you have!

Saying yes against your better judgement to something that you know you want to achieve in a timeframe that seems almost impossible can be thrilling and exciting. The power of the deadline or expectation it creates can invoke productivity and momentum that goes off the usual scale. It forces you to commit, forces you to follow through and, in turn, forces you to say no to lots of other things that will come your way, as you manage the monster you have created.

There are certain times when you need to play to the deadline. Making a public pronouncement that you'll have something ready by a certain time forces a scramble for the line. This is a particularly over-used trick in industries like advertising and marketing, where people throw everything at pleasing clients and meeting deadlines. A little bit of that exhilaration and the occasional late night are fine – I'd argue that they're part of life's rich tapestry of experiences and are to be celebrated – but when they become a regular part of your working routine and the occasional crunches become constant exhaustion and eventual burnout, then it's as far from thrilling as can be.

P is for Procrastination and Power Hours

Procrastination

P: People made Powerless by Pernicious and Problematic Putting-off. Yes, 'P' is of course for procrastination. We need to talk about what you do when you don't know what to do. People procrastinate in a whole host of ways – some obvious, some less obvious – but at the heart of procrastination is one of three causes:

- Fear
- Boredom
- Lack of clarity.

Spotting procrastination in yourself isn't as easy as you think. Yes, we all know when we're on Facebook or surfing the web at work, but there are a whole heap of often subtle signs that you might be procrastinating and putting things off, such as:

- Being a perfectionist

- Arranging a meeting about doing the work you could just do now

- Spending ages changing fonts, styles or titles when the rest of the work is already done

- Spending hours on research or data collection

- Leaving out the controversial or interesting bits

- Over-organizing

- Being afraid of change

- Criticizing people for trying to be innovative or different

- Worrying more about the word count than the words

- Obsessively checking your work

- Asking others for reassurance disguised as feedback

- Making a cup of tea instead of starting a courageous conversation

- Playing with productivity apps on your phone rather than being more productive.

The problem is that a lot of the ways we procrastinate are not that far from being useful and are productive pieces of work in their own right. You'll probably remember how tidy your bedroom was when you were younger and had homework or exam revision to do.

You can overcome the procrastination resulting from a lack of clarity by keeping a really good Master Actions List and being really clear in the language you use with yourself about the next physical actions you need to take. Knowing what needs to be done frees you up to focus on the doing rather than being caught between the thinking and the doing. To some extent, you can also breathe motivation into the things that are boring, either with deadlines or rewards or positive momentum psychology.

However, much harder to deal with is the procrastination that comes from our fear. So let's focus here on where that fear comes from physically and how we can counter it.

The lizard inside of you

When you think of the image of a brain, you tend to think of the cerebral cortex. Underneath that familiar-looking shape is the limbic system, and one of its key components is the amygdala: the 'fear centre' in the brain. It's often nicknamed the 'lizard brain' – a term popularized by Seth Godin's brilliant book, *Linchpin*, because the limbic system pre-dates much of the rest of the brain in terms of human evolution. Put simply, this part of the brain is responsible for survival.

So, what does having a lizard brain mean? Well, it means that you can't hide or dismiss the feelings of fear and the effects of adrenaline – that 'fight or flight' response that you feel when you're under pressure.

Think for a moment about how a lizard survives. It survives by blending in to the background, by viewing the world through a paradigm where every scrap of food that something else eats instead of it is to be jealously resented, and where the purpose of the day is to guard its safe spaces, protect its loved ones and protect its very existence.

Much of our work as knowledge workers involves taking risks and stepping outside of what we know to be comfortable. Yet standing out from the crowd in evolutionary terms meant you'd get picked off by a predator. This is exactly how your lizard brain still thinks!

What Stephen Pressfield refers to as 'the resistance' is a mindset, usually developed by the lizard brain, characterized by stress, anxiety, fear of failure, fear of success and a whole host of other emotions that whir around our brains and tell us to stand still.

'Stop. Don't do it. It's risky. Do it how others do it because that's what we know is already accepted behaviour. Innovation and unorthodoxy is a crazy idea. Creativity is just wrong.'

Sometimes the biggest barrier to productivity, to creativity, to achieving the very things we desire is our own lizard brain. Silencing it is hard, tricking it or getting around it takes practice, and even recognizing it as the root of our paralysis from the task can be difficult. Often, the impulses from your lizard brain are so quiet that you don't even realize they need silencing at all. Pay close attention to yourself and your gut instincts, but also objectively observe your productivity, noticing which tasks you're drawn to and repelled by, which bits of work you can fly through and which things seem to fill you with worry, fear and dread. You don't need to be a psychologist or a counsellor or perform complex analysis on your own thinking, but you do need to pay close attention to it.

Those little voices telling you that your work will likely suck? That's the lizard brain. The impulse to play it safe rather than take the big risk that you know will pay off? That's the lizard brain too. The fear that what you're about to show to your boss or present in front of people or put out into the wider world will be ridiculed? It's all the result of the lizard brain. The larger part of your brain – the bit that deals with the rational and objective thoughts – calculates the likelihood that the lizard brain's nightmare scenarios will come true as being slim-to-none, but somehow the tiny lizard brain still wins.

Power Hours

One way to trick the lizard brain into letting you get on with your work is to acknowledge its need for comfort and safety. Enter the Power Hour.

The idea of the Power Hour is simple. Schedule an hour of your most proactive attention to work on what you're avoiding. After all, it's just an hour of your day. You're free to continue ignoring or stressing or worrying about it for the other 23 hours of your day!

So, think about the thing you're most avoiding, think about the time of the day when you'll have the most proactive attention, and add it to your calendar, just as you would a meeting. Doing this gives it an air of legitimacy: you're fully *allowed* to procrastinate for the rest of the day, as long as you pay the small price of undergoing the Power Hour. And guess what? Once you get started, you usually realize that thing that you were dreading wasn't as bad as you expected, and once you're an hour in, you normally have some momentum to keep it going.

The other way to use Power Hours is to think about this question:

What's the one activity that, if you did it consistently for an hour a day, every day this year, would make a person in your job successful?

If you were a sales person, for example, that activity might be cold calling. If you don't enjoy cold calling, you'll always find something else to do in its place. But developing a habit that every day between 9.30 and 10.30am you cold call will yield fantastic results over time. Most musicians hate doing their scales, most sports people hate warming up, most creative people hate doing the finances and the business administration – but none of these tasks needs to be a huge chore. Often just treating them with a little bit of respect and making them habitual is enough to turn you into the kind of professional that you always wanted to be when you grew up.

Of course, this isn't rocket science. But picture that 'one thing' in your mind right now – the thing that if you do consistently and habitually will make you successful in your job – and the chances are that you're not actually doing it for an hour a day or more.

The Power Hour can be a way to find consistency,

develop muscle, turn a conscious choice into an effortless, unconscious habit and ultimately meet your goals. You'll also find Power Hours easier if you can tell your colleagues you're doing it and ask for their co-operation in not interrupting you during that time.

 OK, let's schedule your very own Power Hour. What time should it take place tomorrow? Will it be the same time every day?

The only two rules are:

1. Once you've committed to a Power Hour, you can't change the time or reschedule it. (You wouldn't reschedule a meeting at short notice with your boss, so why be more willing to let yourself down than you are to let down others?)

2. You can only have one Power Hour each day. The focus on consistently doing one thing well is what counts here.

Q is for Questions

You'll remember earlier in the book we talked about the battle between 'scatter-brained, lazy you' and 'clever, motivated you'. The language that we use with ourselves and the way we motivate ourselves is one of the most important elements of productivity. After all, you can have all the best technology, ideas and plans you like, but if you lack motivation, everything will just stay on the shelf.

All the best coaches in the world know how to ask good questions to induce the right mindset and get people motivated, so honing the right questions will give you the ability to jump out of the slumps. Additionally, it's an important tool for managing your well-being and energy so that you don't push yourself too hard and risk burnout.

How to get questions into your routine

The scatter-brained, lazy part of you doesn't want to hear about questions. Because scatter-brained, lazy you just wants to surf the web, avoid the difficult stuff and coast along until it's time to go home. So, you need to bring questions in as part of your routine. The questions you ask don't need to be habitual or repetitive, but the process of asking yourself good questions does need to be a habit you develop.

There are five natural 'spaces' you can create for questions:

1. Daily questions – which you ask as a ritual at the start of the day

2. Choice point questions – which you ask at the 'choice points' when you're selecting what to do next from your list

3. Weekly questions – which you ask as part of a general weekly checklist (which we'll cover in the 'Weekly Checklist' chapter)

4. Quarterly questions

5. Annual questions.

Coming up with your new year's resolutions usually starts with a period of asking yourself good questions. Whether you do this consciously or subconsciously, the process of writing resolutions – and, in fact, often the reflection period that most people experience before it due to the Christmas holidays – will lead you to think about questions like:

- Am I happy?

- What more do I need in my life?

- What's good or bad right now?

- How can I improve my relationships?

- How much money would I like to make and/or how much do I need to make?

- What are my goals, dreams and aspirations for the year ahead? And what about the year after that, and the year after that?

This process happens quite naturally. It seems at the beginning of the year you're quick to give scatter-brained, lazy you a hard time! Clever, motivated you has your opposite number joining the gym, earning astronomical money, being the ideal parent or child, sailing around the world, driving a better car. It will all change once the clock strikes twelve! Then scatter-brained, lazy you has a few days of winning out because there are good films on the TV, and suddenly clever, motivated you has less of an answer. Well, clever, motivated you doesn't actually need the answers. Clever, motivated you just needs to keep asking consistently good questions, all year round.

You don't need to ask yourself hundreds of questions all the time – in fact, in many ways little and often is the best strategy here – but you should be conscious of the need to throw questions in at some or all of these five points. What follows is not designed to be a prescriptive list. You definitely will not need all of these questions. Perhaps, notice as you read this list which ones excite you or make the clever, motivated version of you smile as you read them, and which ones make the scatter-brained, lazy you recoil in disgust or fear. Choose both of those above the ones that don't elicit as strong a response.

Daily questions (to ask yourself when you first arrive at your desk, on your way to work or over breakfast – whichever way, make it a daily ritual):

- What's in my calendar today?

- What are the three most important things for me to get done today?

- Which of these am I resisting doing? Why?

- How's my energy?

- Which tasks most need my proactive attention, and when is that likely to be?

- Which tasks are dependent on other people, and when can I get their time and attention?

Choice point questions (to ask yourself as you're selecting the next task from your to-do list):

- How's my energy?

- What will I keep thinking about – and stressing about – until it's done?

- What's the quickest way to get this off my desk?

- Is there a precedent here, or a wheel I can avoid reinventing?

- What would a super-efficient 'done' look like here? (Ten minutes? Thirty minutes? Two hours?)

- What are the consequences if I don't do this (if any)?

- Who is nagging me, and how do I quiet them?

Weekly Checklist questions:

- If this project were half the size, what would change?

- What needs me versus what can I give to someone else?

- What is the purpose of this project?

- What will create impact?

Quarterly questions:

- What single thing is my business lacking right now?

- What will create impact?

- Am I staying true to my values?

Annual questions:

- What would be the brave and unexpected thing to do here?

- What needs me and what feeds me?

- What would my heroes choose?

- What makes me excited to get out of bed in the morning?

 Keep a list of the questions somewhere close by or on your home screen, so that you remember to think about them regularly.

R is for Renegotiating, Ruthlessness and Rest

Renegotiating

Times change. And times change your to-do list. Things that you wrote on your Master Actions List or projects that you started a couple of weeks ago might not be as relevant now as they were then. At the same time, we tend to be very quick to beat ourselves up if things aren't getting done. So, as well as taking things off the list because they're finished, it's very useful to get into the habit of renegotiating with yourself. Each week, think about the things that you have to do in the context of what else is going on in the world. It might be that there are opportunities presented elsewhere in your organization for you to 'piggyback' onto certain events or projects, or it might be that your boss's pet agenda last week is something that he's forgotten about now and you probably can too.

Renegotiating your commitments feels odd. It seems somehow counter-intuitive. We might feel guilty about changing our minds and deciding that something is of a lower priority than we thought just a few short weeks ago. But it's important to keep your work and your lists as agile as possible. Changing your mind is not an admission of defeat. It's a recognition that the world isn't static and that you're changing with the times.

Ruthlessness

One of the nine characteristics of the Productivity Ninja is Ruthlessness. To protect your attention, it's important to adopt a ruthless mindset. We've talked already about the art of saying no, but have you thought about your mindset and relationship with tasks you're undertaking versus the ones that are competing for your attention at that same moment?

It's often thought that multi-tasking is a coveted technique to increase productivity. In fact, the opposite is true. 'Mono-tasking' is the way to ruthlessly screen out other distractions so that you can focus on what you're working on. Here are some of the ways you can take steps to be more ruthless with your attention and promote healthy mono-tasking:

- Keep nothing on your desk except paperwork related to the thing you're working on. Other files, paperwork or notes will lead to distraction.

- Don't have other windows or programs open on your screen if you're working on something.

- Go on a low-information diet. Be very choosy about the media you consume and try to avoid any talk radio or TV while you're working on something.

- Get your inbox to zero and then close it down.

- Resist your company's drive towards instant messenger tools (which is even more destructive than your email inbox if you're seeking long periods of mono-tasking!).

- Know when to use the art of Ninja Stealth and Camouflage. Particularly if you work in an open plan office, the propensity to be interrupted is all around you. Leaving your desk and going to a local café or cosy corner of the office where no one can find you is a massive productivity booster.

Ruthlessness also means knowing when to go 'off the grid' and perhaps not playing by the conventional rules. In some companies, the idea of working somewhere out of sight or booking a meeting room just to get yourself out of the crossfire of interruptions might be considered devious or rebellious. However, the design of offices has barely changed in the last fifty years, even though the technology that services them has changed radically.

As someone who visits *a lot* of offices of organizations large and small, my observation is that almost all are set up with the false assumption that open-plan automatically means collaborative, when in actual fact it usually just means destructive noise and interruptions. Even more problematic is that offices tend to be designed for extroverted people (since most organizations like to think of themselves as friendly, exciting and people-driven rather than quiet, 'serious' or overly reflective). So if you happen to be an introvert, your employer is, in this sense, setting you up at a disadvantage to those more comfortable in an extroverted space. My experience is that good managers always respect employees who come to them with suggestions of how they should best work, as long as they can genuinely see that productivity is the central driver of the conversation.

That said, flexibility will only get you so far, and a bit of under the radar Stealth and Camouflage is always a great addition to your repertoire. Think of it as our little secret, OK?

Rest

When you're up against it and burning the midnight oil to finish a project, it's often tempting to keep pushing yourself further and further for days on end. On Saturdays and Sundays, while they might officially be 'days of rest', people are likely sending you emails that are popping up on your phone that you feel an impulse to answer. It's so easy to get caught in the trap that values work above everything else. Yet every study into working hours shows that the more you work, the more you experience diminishing returns from each additional hour. Rest and relaxation is often the most important thing that you can do to boost your own productivity. In the middle of big projects it seems almost counter-intuitive to get an early night when there's so much work still to do, but sleep and rest are such vital components of productivity. Here are five 'sleep hygiene' tips:

1. Studies have found that exercising during the day promotes healthier sleep at night. Even fifteen or twenty minutes of running during the day means that when you get to bed your body is more ready for sleep. However,

don't try to exercise just before bed if you skipped it earlier in the day, as it will wake you up!

2. Establish consistent timings for when you go to bed. Of course, your rules are there to be broken occasionally, but set a hard and fast rule for what time you want to start winding down, what time you'll be in bed by and what time the alarm is set for.

3. Leave talk radio stations, smartphones and tablets out of the bedroom. Make the bedroom a haven of peace and relaxation. Make the only 'media' in your bedroom a good book or relaxing music.

4. Keep a piece of paper beside your bed to Capture and Collect new ideas or things that are 'nags' from existing work. Writing it down tells the brain it's being dealt with. If you don't, it'll likely rattle around your head for hours and wake you up again sometime.

5. Use an app like Sleep Cycle or a wristband device like Fitbit or Jawbone UP when you sleep. What these are able to do is monitor your sleep movements and wake you up at the point that you're already stirring. For example, mine is set to wake me up by 7am at the latest, but if my Jawbone UP senses I'm coming out of a sleep cycle and I'm stirring any time after 6.30am, it'll wake me earlier, which leaves me feeling less groggy when I wake up, even though it's earlier!

S is for Seven Habits

Stephen Covey's *The 7 Habits of Highly Effective People* is one of the seminal books written on the subject of personal development and self-management. Originally published in 1989, it became an instant best-seller, even prompting US President Bill Clinton to call up Covey to invite him to help Clinton integrate his principles into the administration. It's also a book I've returned to several times over the years.

It's far from perfect: some of the specifics of the time management system are a little rigid for many people, not to mention a little dated (let's not forget it was written in the days before email!), and yes, some of the language is a little gung-ho, but some of the key principles are worth revisiting. My view is that no one will ever be perfect at all seven habits, so that means a quick refresher should always be useful!

KEY FIGURE **Stephen Covey** wrote a number of best-selling books, but was best-known for *The 7 Habits of Highly Successful People*, which has sold in excess of 25 million copies since its launch in 1989. He founded what is now FranklinCovey, one of the world's largest management training consultancy firms. He died in 2012 at the age of 79.

The first three habits are all designed to focus on the personal, encouraging independence:

'Habit 1 – Be proactive'

Being proactive is about knowing where you have the ability or authority to take action versus the things that you have no control over. Smart people don't blame their surroundings or make excuses – they learn to accept and react to the things they can't control but to take affirmative action to solve the problems within their control.

'Habit 2 – Begin with the end in mind'

Covey invites you to spend time thinking about your 'personal mission statement'. Imagine being a fly on the wall at your own funeral. What do you want people to be saying about you? What is the mark you've left on the world? Who remembers you, and for which character traits? Thinking about your legacy as being one that you deliberately choose is a great way to delve deeper into your own values and goals. The end point becomes your compass as you make day-to-day decisions.

'Habit 3 – Put first things first'

'Don't prioritize your schedule, schedule priorities' is a fantastic piece of advice. This encourages focus on those 'quiet priorities' that will never be the glaringly urgent things, but that if slotted into the work schedule will pay huge dividends, despite the fact that more urgent problems or tasks might be shouting louder.

Habits 4 to 6 are designed to move you from focussing on the personal to focusing on the interpersonal or interdependent.

'Habit 4 – Think win-win'

Covey talks inspiringly of developing an 'abundance mentality': the idea being that so much of our behaviour in work and in life is driven by a 'zero-sum mentality', where there are scarce resources, everyone is in competition with each other and where if I'm to win, you must lose. The abundance mentality is the ultimate in turning the Gordon Gecko 'greed is good' mantra on its head.

What if, instead of win-lose, we focused on co-operation and win-win? Co-operation is a much better strategy for work and life. When you achieve success or receive resources (both material and emotional), share them and demonstrate that you have more than you need. Like magic, you'll find that you build up goodwill with so many people that their successes are shared with you too. You scratch my back, I'll scratch yours. If you choose only to work or live selfishly, you'll find everyone else will too. But approach problems generously and collaboratively, and you'll find everything is easier, as other co-operative people flock to you and collaborations make things happen.

'Habit 5 – Seek first to understand, then to be understood'

This is probably my favourite of the seven habits. Listening is the most important communication skill there is. Practising 'empathic listening' in your conversations with people is about approaching the world through their frame of reference, not yours. Of course, it's possible to deeply understand someone and have a great handle on the way they see the world, even if you still disagree with them. It's all about diagnosing the situation before you prescribe a solution. And by building emotional as well as intellectual connections, you can explore ideas or problems more collaboratively rather than in opposition. So, next time you're in a conversation with someone, try listening with your eyes and your heart as well as with your ears. You'll be surprised how powerful that can be.

'Habit 6 – Synergize'

OK, so a book that sells millions of copies will have inevitably spawned its fair share of cringe-worthy business-speak. In simple terms, synergize means seeking the areas of shared purpose in a situation and being respectful and mindful that there may also be differences too. Again, it's about working for collaboration and being respectful of others.

The final habit is all about ensuring sustainable self-improvement.

'Habit 7 – Sharpen the saw'

This is most definitely the habit that a lot of people neglect the most: renewal. Covey focuses on four dimensions of renewal: physical, mental, social/emotional and spiritual. He argues that if we don't take some time out to rest and recuperate, we risk burnout. Also, this rest time doubles up as our time to reflect on what we're doing, check our progress and form ideas to improve or change tack. So 'sharpening the saw' is actually what makes the other six habits work well.

I've spent the last year or so becoming obsessed with my habits and how to change them. What I've realized more and more is that changing habits is rarely about acquiring new knowledge: we all generally know what's good for us, and we know that most of that common sense and clichéd stuff does actually work. Similarly, Covey's work often articulates things that we instinctively already knew, but he also tells us that 'just knowing' alone is useless, and inspires us to take some action instead.

T is for Tools

Be Weapon-savvy

Productivity tools come in all kinds of shapes and sizes. 'Thinking tools', such as the CORD Productivity Model, the 40-20-40 continuum for looking at meetings or the email processing framework described in the 'Inbox Zero' chapter, are arguably more powerful than anything you can download to your smartphone because they create the framework from which you can develop and perfect good productivity habits. However, there is no doubt that some of the practical tools, such as apps to manage your lists and programs to help you create great work, can be very important too.

Some people place much more emphasis on tools than others. In fact, there can be a tendency to procrastinate *with* tools – it can be tempting to waste time experimenting with tools, in search of the elusive 'perfect app'. Think of tools not as shiny new playthings, but in the same way any craftsman thinks about his or her tools: once a carpenter owns a good plane and a good lathe, they don't spend hours searching around for another one, they get on with the work. Of course, they might be tempted to look at a colleague's kit with a bit of envy every now and again, but there's only so much additional utility to be gained from any new tool, so save your experimentation for the things that can radically alter how you see the world and give you a much more powerful performance.

For that reason, I'm not going to talk at length about email programs or apps (you're probably using the one you've been given at work, and the one you prefer using for your personal email), and I don't believe there's enough of a difference between Microsoft, Google and Apple's offerings when it comes to word processing and spreadsheets for it to warrant a long discussion here.

However, for what it's worth, and probably quite unfashionably in the world of productivity, I'm a huge fan of Microsoft Outlook, and if I had to choose one email program for the purposes of email processing and getting back to inbox zero as quickly and clearly as possible it would be that.

Remember we said before that a Productivity Ninja is Weapon-savvy. This means that the focus isn't on tools for the sake of having cool tools, it's about making sure that any investment of time in a time-saving app or tool will pay dividends in increasing productivity. Many people are tempted to 'go digital' and invest in apps or expensive software to manage their lists, but if you prefer the analogue approach, good old pen and paper is just fine. There's even a neat trick where you can use the back of your paper notebook for projects and actions, leaving the front clear for your more regular notes from meetings and so on. Use the inside back cover for your Projects List and the inside back page(s) for the Master Actions List – because the Master Actions List by nature will change and need replacing with a new page pretty regularly, whereas the Projects List stays pretty constant, since many of this month's projects are also next month's projects.

Likewise, familiar tools such as Word and Excel are easy to use for lists and can be all you need. Microsoft Outlook's Tasks function is actually a very underrated list-manager – set it up based around the categories view instead of the standard view, and it can be very effective. So, before I talk about smartphone apps, it's worth noting that while such new tools can be great, it's only worth investing the time in setting them up if you really think they're going to be things you'll use regularly.

To-do list apps

Let's start with the most important app category for productivity: the to-do list app you're going to use for your second brain.

Toodledo

This has been the app of choice in the Think Productive office for a while now. It certainly doesn't have the prettiest interface (especially its tablet app, which is quite dull), but the website interface is very easy to use, it synchronizes perfectly between phone and website, and it has everything you need. The web version is free, and the phone and tablet apps are no more than a couple of pounds to buy. Toodledo keeps it simple and functional. It has a lot of functionality (more than most people will use), but you can tailor the fields so that you see the ones you use more prominently first. Remember, the ones you'll need to apply the CORD Productivity Model to are as follows:

- **Master Actions List** – save each action as a 'task', and use the 'context' field to split your list by places, @office, @home, etc.

- **Projects List** – use the 'folder' field. Simply add each action to a folder to create the ability to see everything on a project-by-project basis.

- **Daily To-do List** – you can use the 'priority' field to bring today's actions to the surface, or alternatively simply scribble your Daily To-do List on a sticky note if you like the more tactile, analogue approach!

- **Good Ideas Park** – add a folder called 'Z Good Ideas' so that it sits at the bottom of your projects.

- **Waiting For List** – add a 'context' called 'Waiting' (or 'Z Waiting') so that this list just sits at the bottom of your Master Actions List.

Informant
Informant/Pocket Informant has been around for a while. It synchs perfectly with Toodledo, meaning you can use Toodledo on your phone, but then can see all the same data on Informant's tablet app. Informant has a decent calendar function too, which brings in data from your Google or tablet calendar. It's great when you're reviewing everything.

Nozbe

Nozbe is a slightly more expensive option (running on a monthly subscription of a few pounds a month), but if you're going to use an app regularly, it's worth prioritizing finding the right app. There are better ways to save a few pounds a month than scrimping on the wrong app! It's my own current app of choice, with functionality very similar to those discussed above. In fact, there are fewer settings to choose from than with Toodedo, but where it excels is in being really easy to use. I currently run Nozbe on my phone, an iPad and two separate PCs. There is also a web-based app if I'm ever working on another machine. It synchs the data across all devices beautifully, and on a touchscreen interface, I can drag and drop new tasks into the 'Contexts' section to add them to my Master Action List and drop them into the 'Projects' on my Projects List, so that I can view things project by project. Wherever you go in the app, you're never far away from a big plus symbol, so that it's really easy to add new tasks or ideas whenever you think of them. You can even add stuff to your Nozbe account via email or Twitter.

Todoist

Todoist has many admirers and works on many different platforms. One of Think Productive's Productivity Ninjas, Lee, is a Todoist obsessive. The website has a clear but colourful drag-and-drop design, and its phone and tablet apps are perhaps slightly better than Toodledo's. It also has a really nice range of other features such as plug-ins to integrate directly with different browsers, email systems and calendars. Again, the free account gives you everything you need, and the phone and tablet apps are free too, but there's a subscription of around £18 (around $30) per year for some of the advanced features.

Evernote
Evernote is far and away the most popular 'digital filing cabinet' around. It's fantastic for storing the reference information and other little snippets of digital information that you don't need to complete actions but that you do want to keep. While it's not explicitly a list manager, I have seen people customize Evernote to be a great list manager, alongside all the other cool things that it does.

Back-up/ Cloud storage

Dropbox
Dropbox is the clear winner here. It probably needs no introduction, other than to say if you're one of the few people yet to start using it properly, then you're missing out.

Mindfulness

Headspace
Headspace is not only a great personal tool, but it's what we use at Think Productive for the office's daily meditation. Run by a guy who used to be a Buddhist Monk, it's a friendly

companion to anyone who wants to learn meditation or keep up a daily practice. The main feature on the free version of the app is called 'Take 10' – it takes just ten minutes a day and really makes a difference.

Centering Practice

From the complex to the utterly simple, this app has become a real favourite for me. Recommended by embodiment training specialist Mark Walsh, the app reminds you to take stress-busting pauses from your work. During the pauses, you follow a simple centring process, like a mini-mindfulness exercise, that takes just twenty seconds. Its reminders pop up on your phone at seemingly random times of the day, and you spend just twenty seconds reconnecting with your body and the world around you – forgetting the swirls of stress and ideas buzzing around your head. It's a simple but very effective app. Unfortunately, at the time of press, it is available for iPhone only (whereas pretty much everything else we're talking about in this chapter is available for both iOS and Android operating systems).

Finance

Xero

Xero is a cloud-based finance app which allows you to manage the entire finances of your business online. It's accountant-friendly (in fact, it's recommended by lots of accountants), which if you run a business cuts out a lot of extra work when you come to hand over your end-of-year accounts to your accountants. But it's on the phone app that Xero really comes alive: I can track invoices and balances, do my bank reconciliation on the move, and even take photos of receipts to be automatically added to my expense claims. It also takes your statements and transactions directly from your bank account using a feed, so no more uploading statements!

Expensify

This neat little app allows you to keep track of out-of-pocket expenses, and once you've uploaded all the receipts and data, you can use it to email out expense claims for approval and payment to your boss or clients.

Other useful tools

1Password

There's nothing worse than needing to get stuff done, but being locked out of the app or website because you forgot the password! Well, perhaps the only thing worse than that is using the same password for every single website you visit. Luckily, this neat little app, which you can download onto your computer for a few pounds, will store all of your passwords safely and even auto-generate highly secure passwords for all the sites you use and any new ones you join. To access any site you have an account with, you simply log into your 1Password app, and the app will automatically log in to wherever you want to go from there.

iPadio

iPadio is a great little tool I use to record conference calls or just general audio to listen to again later. Basically, you log in to the app, make the call, and when you finish, iPadio saves the whole thing as a file on its website. (Its idea is that you can make 'instant radio stations', which, to be honest, I don't really understand the need for, but there's an option to set all the files to private, too!)

Website Blocker/ StayFocusd

There are several free Google Chrome extensions that can block websites on which you know you're liable to procrastinate. I personally use Website Blocker to block Facebook during business hours, so I have no access to it at all. You can also use StayFocusd to limit the time you spend on each site, rather than block them completely. Another example of where clever, motivated you can set the rules for scatterbrained, lazy you and help you protect your attention.

U is for Urgent vs. Important

After Stephen Covey covered the theory of 'urgent vs. important' it became a mainstay of management consultancy, but it was originally said to be how former US President Dwight D. Eisenhower organized his tasks.

Urgent vs. Important Matrix

	Urgent	Not urgent
Important	1	2
Not important	3	4

The idea is pretty simple: choose and schedule your work based on which quadrant each of your tasks fits into – things that are:

1. Both urgent and important
2. Important but not urgent
3. Urgent but not important (to us, at least)
4. Not urgent and not important.

The power in this model is where it influences what's happening in quadrants two, three and four. Quadrant one – the stuff that's both urgent and important – is often the stuff that we're reacting to, or is so 'front of mind' that we don't even need to consult a list to think about. Using this model to create the insight and discipline to focus on quadrant two regularly – and prioritizing these important tasks above succumbing to the noise and addiction of the urgent – is a difficult but extremely valuable habit to develop as you're making choices. Likewise, learning to view the things that fall into quadrant four as things you can simply delete or forget about is one very important component of Ninja Ruthlessness.

So the classic urgent versus important matrix is a very useful tool for reminding us of those areas where we may not naturally or easily put our time and attention. I find personally that ranking everything by urgent and important is too cumbersome a technique to use when I'm Organizing my thoughts, actions and projects. But when I'm Reviewing my week's work, it's a great tool to use to get some perspective, to see what I'm doing well and to see what I need to improve. With our priorities shifting more regularly these days and our need for agility, I tend to think of this less as an 'in the moment' tool and more as a tool to reflect on the choices I'm making.

You can, of course, use this tool very literally if you want to: look at what's on your Master Actions List. Rank each item on a scale of one to ten by how important it is. Then, give everything another rank based on how urgent it is. Does this change how you might have tackled the list? What surprises you here about the results?

Let's look at this tool more reflectively. How do you generally fill your days? Email, for example, often falls into the low importance but high urgency quadrant. A common problem we all face is how little time we spend on the high importance but low urgency tasks. These are important goals, but when there is so much to keep us distracted or in fire-fighting mode, it's no wonder that we can spend whole weeks thinking we'll get around to the important goal tasks 'when everything calms down'. Have you ever noticed how that mythical 'next week' when everything is 'back to normal' never actually seems to arrive? There's always some other high-urgency item to drag us away from what matters.

We will come on to look at the Weekly Checklist Review shortly, so you might like to use this tool as one of your weekly 'questions', or just revisit it from time to time when you're reviewing your progress.

V is for Vision

We couldn't near the end of a book like this without asking the biggest question of all: why?

Why do you do what you do? What's your vision? What's your vision for your career? What about for your life and family? What's your ultimate BHAG? What are the values by which you want to live your life and make decisions? What's the change you want to bring about in the world?

These are big questions to answer, and the chances are you might have tweaked and changed how you answer them over the years. But it's worth taking some time to think about your own personal vision.

Here are ten questions that can help you to form your vision:

1. How would I like to be remembered?

2. What sentence would I love to know someone was going to say in my eulogy?

3. Who among my friends and peers do I most admire, and how can I be more like them?

4. What single thing most excites me?

5. What single thing most angers me?

6. What are the things I want my children to learn from me (either now or in the future)?

7. What achievement so far in my life am I most proud of, and why?

8. What story do I know I keep telling myself that I want to stop telling myself?

9. How long will it take to achieve my vision, and what are the steps I need to take along the way?

10. How will I know when I've achieved it?

From these questions, you might start to form your personal BHAGs that we talked about at the beginning of the book. That last question is particularly important: trying to answer how you'll know when you've achieved your vision is a helpful guide to making sure your vision is measurable and achievable enough. For example, 'happiness' is not a good vision, since it's an abstract and elusive concept that you'll never know whether you've reached. A good vision is grounded in realism and clarity, whereas a bad vision feels like chasing butterflies.

You may also find it easier to think about vision when you have an expansive view. It's much easier, for example, to think big, bold and ambitious thoughts when you're staring out over an inspiring skyline rather than locked in a tiny basement meeting room. And it's also much easier to focus on this kind of thinking when you're far away from the day-to-day routine. So, turning off your emails and using some Ninja Stealth and Camouflage to get out of the office or away from regular distractions can be very helpful.

Envisioning the small stuff

There's another way to think about the word 'vision', which is much less grand but no less important for productivity. The CORD Productivity Model asks the question: 'What's the next physical action?' Developing a vision in your mind that sees you undertaking the task can help you to see things more clearly – and can reduce procrastination and uncertainty. The word 'physical' is a very important one here because it forces you to think about how you actually go about completing the task. 'Following up' is not a physical action. You can't physically 'follow up'. Yet 'email' or 'call' or 'have a conversation during the team meeting' are all physical things that you can do.

Likewise, when you feel your lizard brain throwing resistance towards particular tasks – say, running a meeting – envisioning can help to get a clear picture in your mind of the room, the people, the likely conversations, the sights, sounds and smells. Envisioning the entire process can help to boost your confidence about what's to come and to silence the lizard brain's protestations and worries.

W is for Weekly Checklist

Earlier, we looked at the CORD Productivity Model. The 'R' of CORD stands for Review – a productivity habit that is one of the cornerstones of David Allen's *Getting Things Done*. His idea of a 'weekly review' is that you spend some time once a week doing the hard thinking that keeps each of your projects on track. You also use this review time to interact fully with your lists, clearing off any tasks that you've already done and adding on new tasks, so that you make sure that your lists feel up-to-date and are a 100 per cent accurate reflection of your current workload.

Spending time doing a weekly review is a difficult habit for a lot of people to implement for a few key reasons:

- The process itself can be long – usually at least an hour, and some bloggers have even talked about their weekly reviews taking four or five hours.

- It is hard work. By nature you are doing all the difficult thinking in one go, which is strategically a great idea, but unless you attack it with proactive attention and vigour, it can be difficult and tiring.

- It is difficult to justify spending time 'out' from doing the work when you're up against it. Although, ironically, this is also the time when you may benefit most from the perspective that a review brings you.

- It's easy to get out of the habit of doing it and then find that it's been several weeks since your last one. When that happens, a bit like going to the gym, it seems to become cumulatively more difficult to break the cycle.

My suggestion is that regular familiarization with your second brain makes the reviewing process easier. Undertaking a short familiarization with your Master Actions List as part of a daily ritual, along with a more formal, project-based weekly review, brings clarity, calm and the ability to regularly see the 'big picture'.

When done well, a weekly review process is extremely powerful as it allows you to batch up the important project-based thinking that keeps your work on track. It enables you to make great priority decisions that save time and effort, such as renegotiating and reducing your workload, working out easier and quicker ways to achieve the same outcomes and effectively juggling multiple projects by being able to see them all from a high-level perspective. The end of a review feels exhilarating and exciting: you reach a point of having complete clarity over your workload, confidence that you're doing the right thing and a rush of energy towards what's coming up on your to-do list.

What's quite amazing when you experience that level of clarity is that it points out just how habitually 'foggy' we are when we go about our work. We often work on one project with a gnawing doubt that another project probably needs our attention, that something else is probably slipping behind schedule and that there are most likely decisions that we're not making. Regular review begins to eliminate this doubt, and it's not only extremely empowering, but it radically reduces your sense of stress and discomfort in your work.

The joy of checklists

The best way to develop good habits and make reviewing your lists as easy as possible is with a checklist. The purpose of a checklist is to design a process once that you might otherwise need to write or think about over and over again. It captures that thinking so that once you've come up with the perfect process, you don't need to keep rethinking the process every week (and of course you can tweak and adapt your checklist the more you use it). A checklist frees you up to merely complete the process rather than having to remember it. Here are a few good regular checklists that you could develop:

- A beach holiday packing checklist. Packing is so much easier when you have the benefit of hindsight from every other similar holiday you've been on. You'll never forget your swimming gear, insect repellent or travel insurance documents ever again!

- A team meeting agenda checklist. In fact, a checklist is handy for any meeting that reoccurs regularly.

- A Christmas checklist. All the food, people to buy

presents for, things to arrange ... a checklist can take at least some of the stress out of it.

In all of these cases you'll probably be able to get by without the use of a checklist, but the checklist acts like a rocket booster for your limited memory (you can think of it as another corner of your second brain) and means you can go about your business with peace of mind, knowing that nothing will be forgotten and nothing will fall between the cracks. And if it does, it'll only happen once because you can update the checklist! Even when you know a checklist by heart, it helps provide that step-by-step assurance. It's like the feather in Dumbo's hat in the Disney movie: even if you can operate without it, why wouldn't you keep it there for comfort?

IF YOU REMEMBER ONE THING To be clear, these checklists are NOT to-do lists. They are simply the lists of the consistent thinking or behaviours that make up your daily or weekly review time. They may involve some tasks that recur, but they'll also involve things that you just need to think about. They are a weekly or daily insurance policy that ensures you pay attention to the right things.

So how do you develop a Weekly Checklist? And what should be on your Daily Checklist?

Making and using a Weekly Checklist

Here are the five stages of a Weekly Checklist:

1. Get all of your inputs back to zero
2. Get your second brain up-to-date
3. Think ahead
4. Get ready
5. Questions.

Stage one: Get all of your inputs back to zero

Stage one is to check that you're on top of the Capture and Collect and Organize habits of the CORD Productivity Model. It's the time to actually do something with all those notes you made during meetings and the bits of paper or business cards that you've been collecting all week. One of the strengths of the Weekly Checklist is that it gives you a level of consistency in knowing that no matter how chaotic your world becomes, you have time set aside to catch up and get back in control. Depending on how chaotic your week has been, this can take anything from a couple of minutes to half an hour or more, but it's difficult to move on to the later stages of reviewing and thinking ahead if you still have inputs lurking around in need of attention. So, this first stage is about getting everything back together – emails, the notes from your meetings, the new nags and ideas that have come from a busy week, the remembering actions or ideas from conversations with your boss and anything else in between.

Stage two: Get your second brain up-to-date

Stage two is about going through your second brain and making sure it's an accurate representation of what's happening in your world. Are there new projects or actions that you haven't named and recorded? What meetings did you attend and what's coming up? Is there anything that you've yet to capture and turn into an action or a new project?

Stage three: Think ahead

Stage three is where you start to think proactively about each project. What are the next stages? What do you need to start moving forward on? What risks do you need to take? Which projects need a gear change and which need you to apply the brakes?

The thinking done during stages two and three of your Weekly Checklist can be crucial to your entire week. It's the time when your main bits of 'organizational architecture' interact with each other: the Projects List, Master Actions List, Waiting For List and calendar. Each of these four components is fine on its own, but it's bringing them all together that generates confidence, trust and control. Doing this thinking well now allows you to forget about almost everything other than just your Master Actions List and calendar for the next seven days. Everything you need is on your Master Actions List for you to look at each day, and your calendar provides the guide to any time-specific things you need to think about.

Stage four: Get ready

Stage four is all about preparation. Do you have your transport arrangements or tickets sorted out? Print them now and get them into your bag. Do you need to print agendas for meetings? Do you need to make sure you have certain files or bits of paperwork? It's the same mentality as when parents make sure their kids pack their bags for school the night before. It means you can head through the week feeling like you don't have to be distracted by the uncertainties these little tasks might throw up, and it means you spend the week with your attention and focus on the detail of what matters, not on panicking about finding the things you need. When you do this stage well, it makes you feel as if you have your very own out-of-sight personal assistant!

Stage five: Questions

Stage five is about remembering to question what you're doing. So at the end of the review, when you've done all of the hard thinking, when you're up-to-date and feeling ultra-clear about everything you need to do, it's the perfect time to be asking yourself some of those bigger questions.

It's unlikely that two Weekly Checklists would ever be exactly alike, and it's important that you tailor the checklist to your own needs, style and role. However, it's useful to have an idea of what might be covered during each of these five stages. Below is a basic example roughly based on my Weekly Checklist.

Emily Example's Weekly Checklist:

Stage one – Get all my inputs back to zero:
- Email inbox back to zero

- Empty paper in-tray

- Any receipts in my wallet?

- Any notes from meetings in my notebook?

- Any new ideas in my head? (Capture them now!)

Stage two – Get my second brain up-to-date:
- Go through the calendar, one week behind to two weeks ahead

- Any actions or follow-up?

- Go though second brain

- Are my lists up to date?

- Check Waiting For List

- Go through @Waiting and @Action folders on email

Stage three – Think ahead:
- Go through Projects List

- Make sure I have at least one action for every project and add new ones to Master Actions List

- What are my big deadlines or priorities for the week ahead?

- Which tasks are going to need specific time set aside in order to make them happen?

- When will my energy and attention be best next week? What is most appropriate to do in those moments?

Stage four – Get ready:
- Travel plans? Print out the tickets, look up train times, etc. to make it smooth next week.

- Any printing or preparation needed for upcoming meetings?

- Get all the files I need for the week ready on my desk/ in my bag

- People: any people who I need to (re)confirm plans with, or talk to about upcoming plans?

Stage five – Questions:
- Am I feeling resistant towards certain tasks? Why? How can I overcome that?

- What am I going to love or hate this week?

- What can I delete or be ruthless about? Can I renegotiate my commitments to focus only on what creates IMPACT?

- What's going well or badly in my productivity right now? Do I feel like a Productivity Ninja? What should I change?

- How's my diet going? What can I do next week to keep it on track?

- Am I finding time for the people and things I love (outside of work)? If not, make some plans now!

 Use the example checklist to come up with your own personal version. Schedule two hours in your calendar for some time over the next week to try out the checklist and get into the habit of regular review.

The Daily Checklist

The Daily Checklist is much, much shorter by comparison, and a bit of a shallower dive too, since you're not dealing with all the depth and complexity of projects and your overall plate of commitments. Yet the Daily Checklist is no less important. Because while the Weekly Checklist covers the grandiose topics of strategy and prioritizing, all of that would be pointless pontification were it not for the practical obligation of getting stuff done. The Daily Checklist is your daily ritual to prepare you for a day of ruthless, efficient, calm delivery of the stuff that matters. It takes no more than about five minutes and again, focuses on the familiarizing you with what's on your plate so that you can be confident in your decisions.

My own Daily Checklist currently looks like this:

1. How am I feeling? Physically? Mentally? Emotionally?

2. What's in my calendar today, and what deadlines are looming? Who else am I dependent on and what's their schedule like today?

3. Scan my Master Actions List and write my Daily To-do List on a sticky note (reminding myself to be reasonable and not over-ambitious!).

4. Frogs and resistance – what items on the list am I avoiding? Why? How can I change that? What 'frog' am I going to eat first?

5. What tasks will need the most energy and proactive attention today? When should I be doing those?

You may also like to throw in other rituals here. Over the years I've combined my daily to-do list with different things, really just to keep it fresh. I've combined it with the end of my morning run, I've done a few minutes of meditation at the beginning or end of the checklist process, I've done it while eating breakfast, I've done it sat outside during the summer …. You could do it on your journey to work, while you make your morning coffee, or when you're out walking the dog. I've even known people to find a Daily Checklist 'buddy' so that to the rest of the office it looks like they're having a short morning meeting. (Either that or a romantic affair!) Doing this keeps them both accountable and makes sure they do it. The idea really is that it's a few fleeting moments to focus attention on yourself and think about what you want to achieve that day, and how.

Just like with the Weekly Checklist, you'll find you gain a sense of clarity and purpose from those few moments that can last the whole day. In time, it just becomes habitual, and you'll start to feel it on the days when it doesn't happen (when things like an early morning meeting or an overnight travel stay disrupt your normal routine).

 Use the ideas here to develop either a Daily Checklist review, or a more wide-ranging daily morning ritual that will include a quick review of your lists to get yourself feeling grounded and ready for the day ahead, as well as anything else you find useful or energizing in the morning such as a brisk run, your breakfast or a coffee and a snack at your desk.

 You can run through your Daily or Weekly Checklist anywhere and anytime, but it's worth thinking about how you avoid distractions as much as possible. Get out of your email inbox, find somewhere quiet or uninterrupted (this could be your desk half an hour before everyone else arrives, a coffee shop or a long train ride). It's also worth avoiding attempting the Weekly Checklist if you're tired.

X is for Extreme Productivity

Almost everything I've written in this book so far is stuff that I've been using myself in my own productivity for a long time, although I face challenges in implementing everything consistently, just like everyone else.

But what if there's more? What if we're only just scratching the surface with what we could achieve? What if there are whole new horizons to explore? These questions led me to offer myself forward as a human lab rat in 2013. I dedicated the year to conducting an 'extreme productivity experiment' each month on my blog: www.thinkproductive. co.uk/grahams-experiments-summary.

This chapter is about my experiments and more generally about how to experiment with your own habits.

In the industrial age, if you wanted slightly improved productivity you could tinker with the machines. And if you wanted much greater improvements, you could change the shift patterns or get better machines. In the information age, if you want a slight improvement and you have good productivity habits already, you can hone these existing habits to improve a bit more, but if you want radical change you need to be prepared to be radical with your own habits.

Learning from extremes

It becomes difficult for us to think about our habits because they're so engrained in us. Habits are by their nature not remarkable to us. But taking these habits to an extreme, or changing a behaviour to see if it provokes any extreme reactions that have the potential to form new habits is at once a scary, interesting, enlightening and thrilling thing to do. Extreme productivity scenarios are not for everyone – and indeed they don't have to be permanent either – but they can provide lessons that everyone can learn from.

Failure and safety

To be ready to experiment, you have to be ready to fail occasionally. The potential to fail is different in every circumstance, but creating a 'safe space' to make mistakes is the key to any empowerment or innovation process. So before you mess with your habits (and probably your productivity) in search of exciting new lessons, it's worth considering what is allowed to fail and how you'll deal with things screwing up. Personally, at the start of 2013 I was in a good place with my business. I had a great team that took care of the day-to-day stuff and my role was transitioning so that less of my time was spent on customer-facing work (where arguably the 'safe space to make mistakes' is tougher to carve out).

Once you know you have room to fail, come up with the things you'd like to test. I wanted to do twelve experiments – one for each month of the year – that each explored a different aspect of productivity. Most of them started or developed from a gut feeling or a frustration, asking the question, 'What if I could do this a different way?' or 'What if my assumptions about this aren't right?' Asking good questions is very important when experimenting.

Next, change the rules, or make some up. To test your own habits, you need to live by new rules and watch what happens when you fight with your self-imposed rules to get back to what's comfortable. My rules were always posted on my blog at the start of the month to make it harder to cheat, but you could just as easily share it with the person you sit next to at work, or your team or someone you live with.

Finally, you sit back and enjoy the show. Experimenting with your own productivity habits can be extremely rewarding and exciting. But beware that it has its pitfalls and moments of despair too. So treat everything as a learning opportunity, try not to get hung up on the failures (they're par for the course) and you'll see things in whole new ways.

So, here are the ten biggest lessons that came out of my year of productivity experiments. You can try them for yourself, or come up with your own.

1. Any form of action trumps indecision

My theory here was that we get pointlessly hung up on decision making, often at the expense of momentum. So, I spent a month making decisions by the throw of a dice. Whenever I was unsure what to do, I would ask the dice. It forced me to think of other options and it helped me embrace imperfection and detach my ego from the decisions.

2. Most email is meaningless

I spent a month doing an experiment called 'Email Fridays' (the opposite of those 'no email Fridays'!). Basically, I went completely email-free from Saturday through until Thursday. People I spoke to about it thought I was insane, but nothing major went wrong, and I got so much more creative work done. Emailing once a week did present a few logistical issues, but I'm now emailing either once a day or twice a week, depending on what's happening in my world.

3. Sometimes it's OK to just 'be'

For a month, I worked only one hour a day: 9–10am. I squeezed my working life into seven hours a week. Honestly, this wasn't really sustainable, and I know I was only able to do this because I'm the boss, but I did learn to slow down the rest of the time – reading in coffee shops, going for walks and just living at a more civilized pace than usual. I found it hard to justify (you might agree!) and even harder to do, but it taught me valuable lesson: I hadn't realized how fast I was going.

4. Focus is a muscle you can develop

I practiced meditation in the office, sometimes for ten minutes every hour, sometimes in slightly longer bursts but only once a day. I found that I felt more focused, was less easily distracted, and my work gathered better momentum the more I spent time in the moment.

5. Being stressed encourages behaviours that encourage stress

In a way, this was the opposite of a productivity experiment. I spent the month of May experiencing 'Maynia': living without any of my usual productivity systems, and deliberately not practicing any of the things I preach. I found that I was immediately drawn towards the 'purposefully pointless' things such as checking email or the news or picking up free newspapers, which I usually avoid. During this month I suddenly started to need them to help distract me from the stress I was feeling! It reinforced to me that momentum can spiral downwards just as easily as it can upwards.

6. You can get as much done in four hours a day as you can in eight

I flipped the 9–5 by working 5–9 instead. I worked 5–9pm for some of this and also tried 5–9am. To my eternal surprise, it was the morning 5–9am shift that proved much more productive, and it also meant I could clock OFF at 9am. Beautiful! What was important in that month was that four hours a day forces ruthlessness – I outsourced my email, delegated more and said no to a lot more things. But did anything really important get screwed up or not happen? No, not at all. And I achieved as much in a four-hour day as I normally did in eight. I will definitely be returning to this idea more regularly. Seven, eight and nine-hour work days? I'm beginning to think we've got it all wrong.

7. The body and nutrition matter, but can also be a distraction

I spent a month eating a pre-prepared diet with optimum nutritional value for productivity. I then contrasted this by fasting for Ramadan for a few days, just to see the other side of things. You probably won't be surprised to learn that at times when I was fasting, I was desperate to drink some water and eat some food, and my low blood sugar meant I was finding certain tasks difficult (as well as being a bit 'ratty'). But there was also a certain peace to being awake all day without food and I valued the time I regained by not getting up every half an hour to grab a snack or a drink. You'll also not be surprised to learn that when eating an optimum diet, your attention and focus last later in the day than usual. Fuel for the mind really matters.

8. When you disconnect from tech, you reconnect with yourself

I spent a month living in what I called 'the abyss'. I created a completely internet-free environment for myself, where my phone was no longer smart, where my Kindle and iPad no longer had Wi-Fi connection, and where pen and paper took over from my laptop. Aside from the world slowing down, I felt like the volume and colour turned up slightly – my appreciation for nature, human relationships and the world around me improved. The month allowed me to reconnect with what mattered most to me, and while I (deliberately) wasn't productive during the month, I had several ideas about my work that will be influential for years to come.

9. When life gives you lemons, you have to make lemonade

In the ninth month of my productivity experiments I had to massively change my schedule after my wife and I discovered our unborn child had some complications. I had to cancel a lot of travel and speaking plans, and I didn't know whether to continue with an experiment at all. In the end I decided to focus on what was true and I changed my experiment that month to be called 'the lemon' – exploring productivity when bad things happen. Ironically, it's times when everything else is in the balance that you most question the day-to-day realities you've constructed. And I learned that even in such trying circumstances, there are great lessons in what's important to you – as long as you're looking for them.

10. Kindness is an underrated productivity weapon

With my trials and tribulations continuing and the Think Productive team stretched, I started to think about what we needed to reduce our stress levels. We all had great productivity habits already so there was limited scope for quick wins. What we really needed was kindness. So I booked massages for the team, we had more conversations about what would help each other out, and I made the conscious decision to be kind to myself and model this as a leader.

Instead of beating myself up for being distracted by our baby issues and working into the night to make up for it, I grabbed a beer and watched a movie. Instead of feeling frustrated about what wasn't done, I focused on being thankful for what was around me. And do you know what? I learnt that the mindset of abundance is a far more productive mindset than the psychology of fear and competition.

So even when you think you've got 'productivity' well and truly cracked, let this be a whisper in your ear: there's always more. A year ago that very notion of 'there's always more' probably would have made me downhearted, impatient or frustrated that I was yet to reach the holy grail of perfect productivity. But knowing what I know now, it has the opposite effect on me. Because when you forget about a mythical destination and just relax and enjoy the journey, you learn, grow and experience so much more. And you realize that productivity isn't some kind of chore or a means to an end, it's a beautiful learning experience in and of itself.

REMEMBER THIS!!! I deliberately picked challenging, unrealistic and unsustainable scenarios to explore. Why? Because I think the opportunities for learning are bigger when you push things to the limits. I tried these things so that you don't have to. Try these things if you want, but I'm certainly not telling you that you should.

Y is for 'Yes, and ...'

Resilience and the ability to make something of even the worst situation are undeniably important skills in an age where the only constant is change, and where things seem to change faster than ever before. In thinking about resilience, who can we learn from? Well, think about the things that set your lizard brain off most. Public speaking is often said to be something many people fear more than death. So imagine adding the pressure to be funny into that mix. And the fact that you're on stage, in a play with no script and no one knows what's going to happen next. Welcome to the world of improvisation and improvised comedy. One of the rules of improvisation is the rule of 'yes, and ...', which is all about accepting what your fellow performers or the situation offers to you, and then building on that even further. So we're going to explore the way these two simple words can change the way you react to opportunities and threats.

Improvisation is often most associated with comedy or with the films of people like Mike Leigh, where the dialogue is improvised in the moment by the actors, rather than learned in a script in advance. But it has a much wider application: life itself. So much of our lives are improvised. Often within the stories of those that achieve high levels of success are tales not of meticulous planning but of people making their own luck, of hitting on a gem of an idea – often quite accidentally – and developing it into something bigger. Or people find strength and courage from adverse situations and use those moments to elevate them to somewhere better.

Improvisation may seem hilariously chaotic – and chaotically hilarious – on stage or screen, but underpinning that are a series of rules that the improviser uses to guide their actions and create something out of absolutely nothing, or to rescue a part of the performance that's not going well, all under the pressure of the lights and the audience.

One of these rules is the rule of, 'Yes, and …' It's something you can apply to your own work when you're under pressure, when you need to see things a bit differently or react quickly to something that's happening out there in the wider world.

Saying yes

We talked earlier about the need to ruthlessly say no to certain tasks and demands. So saying yes here is not so much about saying yes to tasks, but about accepting realities. There are good realities and bad realities, sometimes on the same project. For example, a new government-funded programme is offering to give you two free members of staff for the next six months, but the deadline for the application is this coming Friday. You can choose to ignore it completely, or you can choose to accept this exciting reality, think quickly and think big about what opportunities this presents. Or maybe one of your biggest customers or suppliers has just announced that they're going out of business and it's going to radically affect your entire company. These are moments that call for resilience, and the first stage of being resilient is accepting the situation – saying yes and accepting this new truth or reality. That certainly beats mourning for what used to be or clinging on to what we'd prefer it to look like instead. It allows you to nimbly shift your focus to what you actually have to do.

Adding the 'and ...'

So we've said yes and absorbed the new situation we find ourselves in. Now we add the 'and ...' The 'and ...' is about not just accepting the reality but quickly becoming part of it, so that you can build on it further.

The big new opportunity. And? 'We could do *this*!' 'Although it was a surprise, let's embrace this and act quickly to grow the opportunity even further!'

The terrible event. And? 'Well, OK, I suppose we could change things like this.' 'And actually, that would allow us to think more about this other thing we've never got round to.' 'Yes! And actually right under our noses we have the perfect person to do this new thing ...'

Accepting and building. That's the key to making something funny or interesting on a stage when you're making it up as you go along, and when you think about it, we're making up our whole lives as we go along.

There's no script telling you that you need to read this book right now, or hand your notice in at work, or not hand your notice in at work. We may feel like our life has a spiritual purpose or that living by a certain set of values is important to us. But there's no script to guide this reality – we are empowered (either by ourselves or our beliefs) to make things happen by reacting to what's around us. Accept and build. Sometimes we may feel trapped by certain realities, too. And, of course, we have all kinds of inner monologues that can convince us that there's a script even when there is no such thing. But when you realize that everyone else is making it up as they go along too, it becomes comforting and even empowering.

Those who achieve success or make a difference aren't always those with the greatest intelligence or skill; in fact, they're usually those that react quickest and best to what happens to them. They accept, they build. And you can too. Practise saying, 'Yes, and ...' in all kinds of positive or negative situations. You'll be amazed at the transformative power of those two tiny words – and how much time you save by not panicking or procrastinating when new things come along.

 Think back to some recent crisis moments or unusual developments in your work and life. How could the rigorous practising of the 'Yes, and ...' principle have helped, changed or developed those scenarios?

Firstly, think about a time when something went wrong. How could your swift acceptance of the situation have led you to build something better from it more quickly? Or solve the problem completely? Or make lemonade from the lemons?

Think about a surprise new opportunity that's come along recently. How could 'yes, and ...' bring about more creative ideas and help you take maximum advantage?

Z is for Zen

There are many ways to define Zen, a word that has evolved beyond its original roots in Buddhism. Most literally, it describes a meditative state, which in turn invokes the idea of being conscious of the present and living 'in the moment'. So, in this final chapter, we're going to look briefly at the why meditation and being in the moment are vital for anyone interested in productivity, happiness and well-being, regardless of religion.

Mindfulness meditation and productivity

Meditation can often be surrounded by an unnecessary level of mystery or mysticism. However, the principles of mindfulness meditation are surprisingly simple. There's no equipment needed (although a comfy pillow or mattress helps), you can learn how to do it in two minutes, and there are even apps that offer guided mindfulness meditations and provide motivation to help you develop the habit.

If you've never experienced meditation before and don't know where to start, download an app such as Buddhify or Headspace to your phone to get a simple, guided introduction.

What has this got to do with productivity? Well, just about

everything. Since productivity is a result of how we apply our attention and how we deal with our proactive attention as a precious resource, we can use meditation to help us develop a better understanding of what goes on in our brains.

Mindfulness – the ability to pay attention to our minds and feelings in the present moment – is something that can benefit us whether we are meditating or not, and whether our goal is increased productivity or something broader such as mental well-being or happiness. Through meditation practice, we can become more aware of the present moment, which in turn enables a greater focus and the ability to screen out some of the distractions that come from both internal and external sources.

Capturing to stay in the moment

One of the nine characteristics of the Productivity Ninja is Zen-like Calm. The idea is that to be fully engaged with a particular task, you need to be interacting with only that single task, not thinking about the other twenty things you're not doing at that moment, or letting your lizard brain worry about the potential implications of getting it wrong. Zen-like Calm is what psychologists call the 'flow state', where you are totally absorbed in the moment and in whatever you're making happen, right here, right now. What's fascinating to me is that when you're up against a deadline, everything else falls away and you can experience this flow state and its super-productivity quite easily. Many people think it's the deadline that makes them productive, but actually what contributes such a huge bang for your buck is the elimination of distractions and the ability to live in the moment. Developing mindfulness through meditation practice, and seeing this trickle into a greater awareness and a greater ability to be present in whatever you're doing, regardless of deadlines, is very powerful indeed.

Of course, as you work on something, it's also very natural for your brain to trigger reminders of other stuff that needs to be done – perhaps even things that are not currently on your list. But while you can't control the thought, you can control what you do with it. Developing your habit around 'Capturing and Collecting', as discussed in the CORD Productivity Model chapter can massively aid your ability to stay in the moment. You can do this by turning on your to-do list app and having it close by as you work, or simply by having a stack of paper notelets or a mini paper pad on your desk at all times. Then when these thoughts, nags and ideas try to interrupt your flow, you capture them. But more than that, you capture them in the knowledge that they won't be lost by your second brain and that you fully intend to do something with each and every one of those ideas and nags (even if the thing you end up doing is realizing that they were silly ideas and chucking that piece of paper away). The art of Capturing and Collecting is a very mindful and Zen-like process: you acknowledge thoughts as they arrive, and rather than fight them or dismiss them, you try to move beyond them, back to the present moment and onto what matters to you. You can return to those thoughts and the plans that they relate to at some later point. What's important is that your habits are well-honed to give you the confidence to trust that that's exactly what will happen.

Final thoughts

Just as attention is, for me, the most natural place to start a book about productivity, Zen is the most fitting place to conclude it.

Thinking about productivity in terms of our ability to apply our attention to the present moment and to be 100 per cent present with the one thing we're working on or thinking about at any one time unearths a beautiful contradiction: even great planning is the opposite of doing. And doing is the opposite of planning.

It's often tempting – and stress-inducing – to try to multi-task or have our mind wander to more planning or thinking while we're also trying to get something done. It's hard to develop the single-minded and disciplined focus to stay in each moment and stay true to our intention. And we all have our preferences and individual working styles that make something that's hard for me easy for you, and vice versa.

The truth is that productivity is reliant on both in equal measure: the thinking and the doing. We rarely excel at these things naturally, as flawed human beings, and even more rarely does one person excel naturally at both sides of the coin. That's why productivity is such a fascinating subject for me: because each of us has our challenges and there's a learning opportunity around every corner.

And I also like to think that what's true for productivity is also a good lesson for life: ignore the future. Forget the past. Be present in – and make the most of – each and every moment.

Time for some reflection. Think back over the course of this book:

- Are there things you've already started to change?

- What's on your list to try next?

- Are there things you like the sound of but are reluctant to try? If so, I would urge you to spend some time thinking about why, and see if you can challenge yourself to overcome the resistance or think about it in a different way.

- What changes or new habits will turn you into a Productivity Ninja?

- What are your 'next physical actions'?

Finally, having spent this time reading about productivity, it's now over to you. What are you going to do next?

Acknowledgements

Thanks to Kate Hewson, my brilliant editor at Icon Books, without whom many of the sentences in the book would be back to front. Also to Philip and the whole team at Icon, first for approaching me about this project and for subsequently helping me make *How to be a Productivity Ninja* an international best-seller too.

Thanks also to an amazing team of volunteer book reviewers, who gave up their time to read through the first draft and offer feedback: Jen Lowthrop, Julie Bond, Louise Drake, James Hulme, Michelle McGuire, Chris Dubery, Jo Walters, Lee Cottier, Maurice McLeod and Grace Marshall all provided insightful and practical contributions that were instrumental in shaping the final version.

Thanks to the Think Productive 'Ninja family' in the UK and around the world, who keep me inspired and get me thinking about productivity in different ways every day.

Finally, thanks to Chaz and Roscoe for keeping me sane through the process. When I wrote *How to be a Productivity Ninja*, I did so in complete silence and solitude, working from a beautiful beach hut in Sri Lanka. For this one I stayed home. Having the people you love the most in the world within earshot in the next room is quite possibly the very definition of productivity distraction – and it certainly took longer this way! – but there was nowhere else I'd rather have been. Thank you for making every day special.

A–Z of further reading

Attention

Cameron, Julia (1994) *The Artist's Way: A Course in Discovering and Recovering Your Creative Self*, London: Pan Books.

Allcott, Graham (2012) *How to be a Productivity Ninja*, London: Icon Books Ltd.

BHAGs and Batching

Collins, Jim C. and Jerry I. Porras (1994) *Built to Last: Successful Habits of Visionary Companies*, New York: HarperCollins Publishers Inc.

Wikipedia entry on 'Big Hairy Audacious Goal': http://en.wikipedia.org/wiki/Big_Hairy_Audacious_Goal

CORD Productivity Model

How to be a Productivity Ninja, see **Attention**.

Decisions and Distractions

D was for distractions, so we won't give you an extra distraction here!

Email Etiquette

http://five.sentenc.es/

Shipley, David and Will Schwalbe (2007) *Send: The How, Why, When and When Not of Email*, New York: Alfred A. Knopf.

Foibles and Frogs
Tracey, Brian (2007) *Eat that Frog*, San Francisco: Berrett-Koehler.

Buckingham, Marcus and Donald O. Clifton (2004) *Now, Discover Your Strengths*, London: Pocket Books.

Getting Things Done
Allen, David (2008) *Making It All Work: Winning at the Game of Work and the Business of Life*, London: Piatkus Books Ltd.

Allen, David (2001) *Getting Things Done: How to Achieve Stress-free Productivity*, London: Piatkus Books Ltd.

You can see David Allen in action, giving a talk in October 2007 at Google, entitled 'GTD and the Two Keys to Sustaining a Healthy Life and Workstyle': https://www.youtube.com/watch?v=Qo7vUdKTlhk

Habits
Pressfield, Stephen (2002) *The War of Art*, New York: Black Irish Entertainment LLC.

Inbox Zero
You can see Merlin Mann talking about 'Inbox Zero' in a Google talk from July 2007: https://www.youtube.com/watch?v=z9UjeTMb3Yk

43 Folders is Merlin Mann's website on finding time and attention: www.43folders.com

Juice
Loehr, Jim and Tony Schwartz (2003) *The Power of Full Engagement: Managing Energy, Not Time, Is the Key to High Performance and Personal Renewal*, New York: The Free Press.

Kitchen Timers and Keyboard Shortcuts
Cirillo, Francesco (2009) *The Pomodoro Technique: Do More and Have Fun with Time Management*, Berlin: FC Garage GmbH.

The Pomodoro Technique website: http://pomodorotechnique.com

A database of keyboard shortcuts: http://www.shortcutworld.com

Lists
How to be a Productivity Ninja, see **Attention**.

Meetings
Graessle, Lois, George Gawlinski and Martin Farrell (2008) *Meeting Together*, London: Planning Together Associates.

Ninja
How to be a Productivity Ninja, see **Attention**.
The War of Art, see **Habits**.

Over-promising
Saunders, Elizabeth Grace, 'Setting Boundaries and Saying No ... Nicely', *99U.com*, http://99u.com/articles/7076/setting-boundaries-saying-no-nicely

Procrastination and Power Hours
Godin, Seth (2010) *Linchpin: Are You Indispensable? How to Drive your Career and Create a Remarkable Future*, London: Piatkus Books Ltd.

Questions
Stewart, Julia, '101 Incredible Coaching Questions', School of Coaching Mastery blog, http://www.schoolofcoachingmastery.com/coaching-blog/bid/54576/101-Incredible-Coaching-Questions

Renegotiation, Ruthlessness and Rest
'Trouble sleeping? How to sleep like a Productivity Ninja', Think Productive blog, 6 August 2012, http://thinkproductive.co.uk/how-to-sleep-like-a-productivity-ninja/

Seven Habits
Covey, Stephen R. (1989) *The Seven Habits of Highly Effective People*, London: Simon & Schuster UK Ltd.

Tools
A great site for evaluating new tools: www.lifehacker.com

Urgent vs. Important
Hyatt, Michael, 'Is That Task Important or Merely Urgent?', MichaelHyatt.com, http://michaelhyatt.com/is-that-task-important-or-merely-urgent.html

Vision
Look inside yourself – not to others – to create your vision. So, there's nothing to see here!

Weekly Checklist
Gawande, Atul (2010) *The Checklist Manifesto*, London: Profile Books Ltd.

X – Extreme Productivity
Here you can find all the entries from Graham's Productivity Experiments: http://www.thinkproductive.co.uk/grahams-experiments-summary

'Yes, and ...'
The Maydays – Graham's improvised comedy teachers, based in London and Brighton, UK: http://www.themaydays.co.uk/

Zen
http://zenhabits.net/

think productive

If you or your company would like some help with improving productivity, you can contact Graham's company, Think Productive, who will be happy to help!

Think Productive runs a range of public workshops as well as practical in-house workshops for major companies around the world. Popular titles include:

- 'Getting Your Inbox to Zero'
- 'Email Etiquette'
- 'Stress Less, Achieve More' (which helps people implement the CORD productivity model in a day)
- 'How to be a Productivity Ninja'
- 'Making Meetings Magic'

For more information,
email **hello@thinkproductive.com**
or visit **www.thinkproductive.com**

You can reach Graham personally at
graham@thinkproductive.co.uk

Index